1 8

MUM IN A MILLION

MUM IN A MILLION

AKA She Who Must Be Obeyed

Judith Holder

The right of Judith Holder to be identified as the author of this work has been asserted in accordance with the Copyright, Designs and Patents Act 1988.

First published in Great Britain in 2012 by Orion Books
An imprint of the Orion Publishing Group Ltd
Orion House, 5 Upper St Martin's Lane,
London, WC2H 9EA
An Hachette Livre Company

1 3 5 7 9 10 8 6 4 2

A CIP catalogue record for this book
is available from the British Library.

ISBN-13   978 1 4091 4058 0

Typeset by Goldust Design
Printed and bound by CPI Group (UK) Ltd,
Croydon CR0 4YY

The Orion Publishing Group's policy is to use papers that are natural, renewable and recyclable products and made from wood grown in sustainable forests. The logging and manufacturing processes are expected to conform to the environmental regulations of the country of origin.

www.orionbooks.co.uk

This book is dedicated to all mothers everywhere,
without whom the world would be an untidier place
(but a lot more relaxing)

Acknowledgements

Thanks to Charly Conquest whose wit and creativity have helped me enormously, to my truly fabulous partner in crime Jenny Éclair, to Deborah Brown, Judith Derbyshire, Jane Kelly, Christine Skouby, Jill Scrimshaw, and to my two lovely daughters Siena and Ellen who have had to put up with my motherhood all these years. Sorry about that.

Finally, what a shame my own wonderful mother Jean Holder didn't live to see this little book. It would have made her laugh, and a little bit cross with me too.

A-Z
OF MOTHERHOOD

A is for Anything you can do she can do better.

B is for Busybodies – why do you think mums hoover under beds?

C is for Catastrophising – mothers live in a state of high anxiety unless their children are tucked up in bed upstairs and even then they have to go and check.

D is for Disappointment – mostly in the man she married.

E is for Excessive cleaning disorder – she is incapable of leaving the house without the beds being made, a wash on, and the work surfaces wiped. Like anyone else gives a shit. (She's obsessed about dusters, dishcloths, mops, sponges and other pointless items, and tragically knows the difference between each one.)

F is for Fetch me my purse while you're upstairs.

G is for Getting on – whatever you do, never stop a mother getting on, especially with her to do list … mothers have too much to do all the time, or they like to pretend they do.

H Her mess is OK, other people's isn't.

I is for I could kill Nigella.

J is for Juggling – everyone else is just busy. Mothers juggle, apparently.

K is for Know-it-alls – she's been there, done that, got the T-shirt … and that's quite annoying.

L is for Little Jobs – as in 'There are some little jobs I need doing …' The art of delegation is one that mothers have perfected. Cleverer still they go on pamper days and complain how busy they are.

M is for Mum porn – as in articles about people with congenital deformities, royal wedding anything, weight-loss breakthroughs or kittens, catalogues and customer feedback questionnaires …

N is for Not under my roof.

O is for Organising others – whether they want to be organised or not.

P is for the Parking tickets she gets and forbids the kids to tell Dad about.

Q is for Quickly – her only speed.

R is for Recreational drugs for mums – i.e. peppermint tea, Nytol, the Lakeland catalogue and dry white wine.

S is for She who must be obeyed at all times – it's for your own good.

T is for Time – mum time. She calls you at 7 a.m. If she's up, you must be up.

U is for Umbrella. Have you got one with you?

V is for the Voice in your head that sounds just like your mother.

W is for What are you doing inside on a lovely day like today?

X is for extra large – mum pants.

Y is for You'll miss me when I'm gone.

Z is for Zzzzzzzz – mum heaven.

MOTHERHOOD CAN REALLY MESS UP YOUR HAIR

No one prepares you for how hard motherhood is. They try, but you don't listen because you've seen those lovely party dresses for one-year-olds with matching pom-pom shoes in Accessorize. You wouldn't believe them anyway; you'd assume they were being drama queens if they told you that from the moment you give birth and become a mother, your life is no longer your own. I mean, it's fantastic and mums wouldn't want it any other way, but it's no longer about you. Never again will you go to the cinema on a rainy afternoon; never again will you pass Tesco's without thinking, well, I could do with some rinse-aid and while I'm there I'll buy a new mop head; never again will you be able to go to a party and have so much fun you decide to get in the car and drive to Brighton to watch the sun come up; and never again will you go on holiday, lie back and relax unless … it's 'your turn'.

Luckily, God prepares mothers for this total rethink of our lives by giving us first pregnancy then childbirth, both of which mess up your hair big time. After that, anything would seem like a party. It's not as if any of it should come as a surprise: you've seen photos of your own mother before she was pregnant – she was a

13

good-looking woman. Well, kind of; her dress and hairstyle were obviously laughably wrong, but nonetheless she was in reasonably good shape. Then – like the before and after photos in a *Grazia* makeover, but in reverse – your mum got pregnant and, seemingly overnight, blobbed out.

Once you're pregnant, people start using code to describe the way you look as a mother-to-be:

✿ **You look radiant** – they mean nauseous
✿ **You're blossoming** – they mean round
✿ **You look well** – which in all circumstances, pregnant or not, means fat
✿ **You have that pregnancy glow** – means they're not sure what to say that's not 'You look like you need a week off work'.

First comes the nausea. At first you think it might be something you ate – which in my case meant there were quite a few candidates – and yet it doesn't stop you wanting to eat … odd.

Your period's late. You feel like you are heading for the biggest, vilest, heaviest period in the history of womankind, your PMT is so bad you could rip your partner's hair out, everything is pissing you off and making you annoyed and tired and fed up. It's the time of the month, but then again it isn't. Because no period turns up. Nausea turns to the sort of tiredness that leads to you falling asleep in the middle of your own sentences and having an overwhelming need to sleep once fed after 6 p.m. You struggle to keep your eyes open in every meeting you go to. Which is no shift in attitude but suddenly embarrassingly obvious. It's God's way of telling you that for the next nine months you need all the sleep you can get because it is going to be in seriously short supply. Your boobs feel heavy, they're poking over the top of your bra, which seems to be rubbing and giving you jogger's nipple without any of the jogging. You look pale, you're sick in a lay-by on the way home from work. No one else seems to have succumbed to the same food poisoning.

But there's one person who's guessed why – your own mother, of course.

You've been invaded. The alien takes root. You are so large you can barely get yourself behind the steering wheel. You need a sit-down on one of those chairs by the till at the supermarket, and your side of the bed looks like it might collapse under the weight. Luckily, this means you're ready for whatever process you have to go through to get the alien out – or at least you think you are.

Giving birth

Motherhood is a wonderful thing, but childbirth is the toughest recruitment programme on earth, and then some. There's no way to adequately describe the pain of it, though many have tried. It's like someone holding a lighter against your front-bottom/pushing a watermelon out of a hole the size of a grape/pooing a rugby football covered in pins ... Interestingly, your own mother will dodge the issue and tell you that you'll forget about it instantly. Which is her way of saying, This is one thing I can't try to change for you. And that's shocking in itself.

As mothers, all we can do is to try to find ways of discouraging our daughters from going through it too young ...

An adolescent daughter tells her mother, 'Mum, we've been studying sex education and childbirth in school, and I'm a bit worried about the whole thing. I mean, is it terribly painful to have a baby?'

'Well,' her mother replies, 'I'll give you an idea of how painful it is and you can judge for yourself. Put your top lip between your teeth and bite down like you're chewing on a piece of gum ...'

The daughter complies. 'Oh, well that's not too bad.'

'OK,' continues her mother, **'now pull your lower lip all the way over the back of your head like a shower cap!'**

On top of the pain, no one warns you about the indignities of giving birth, which include the following:

❀ **Farting** – three doctors, and your partner will be party to all your gaseous exploits.

❀ **Gas and air** – some mums are in a 'very happy place' when giving birth. One mum asked if she'd had a boy or a girl – when half the baby was still inside her. Another looked down and said, 'That's where they come from?'

❀ **Stitches** – Again, not something you see on an 'It's a girl!' card in Clinton's, although you'd have to applaud them if they did bring out a 'Just the five stitches' range.

❀ **Breaking waters** – think in litres. Think water cannon. It goes everywhere.

Motherhood has been around for a while (even before St Hallmark came up with the brilliant idea of Mother's Day) but we have Eve and her inability to resist apples to thank for being the gender lumbered with childbirth itself.

> *Timothy 2:13–15, For Adam was formed first, then Eve. And Adam was not the one deceived; it was the woman who was deceived and became a sinner. But women will be saved through childbearing – if they continue in faith, love and holiness with propriety.*

Now sinning for chocolate I could understand, but all for an apple? It was probably quite a disappointing apple anyway. They usually are. If it wasn't for this stupid apple, men might have copped for childbearing. Surely women should have had a toss-up, fair and square; best of three, say, or even a penalty shoot-out? But no – all this agony because one woman couldn't resist a Cox's pippin.

Perhaps it's for the best. Men would have made a huge drama out of giving birth. What a strange idea that is: they'd have to go off to do it on their own, in a macho, 'I can handle it' sort of way; birthing plans would involve nominating which beer they would like as pain relief; they'd have to make it competitive, there'd be leader boards and trophies involved. They'd give birth and then feel they had to show off about how bloody hard they'd been. They'd swing baby by its hair in a manly, cavemanlike fashion – and probably want to dress the newborn in high-viz jackets. If men were mothers I am guessing that nappies would be changed less frequently, children would be given chocolate cake for breakfast (they'd argue it does have eggs in) and bedtime would just rumble on all evening because they wouldn't be able to tear themselves away from the cricket. If men were mothers the whole business of motherhood would be uncomplicated – as in, not really thought through but perfectly acceptable. Like soldiers on a battlefield, babies would be left to sleep where they fell, whether that's on the rug in front of the fire or in the armchair. They'd probably forget to put them to bed at all, actually. Clothes would be taken out of the laundry basket, Febrezed and worn again. No school project would be handed in on time and no school uniform would have name tags sewn in or ever be ironed again. Funnily enough, I can see it working quite well. I know no children who wouldn't actually prefer it as a regime.

Motherhood is a closed shop. Plain and simple. No childbirth, no badge. It seems like such a good idea at the time – until, that is, you get to the labour room, experience contractions, and all of a sudden you know what it must be like to have a car reverse over your stomach again and again at regular intervals. Then it seems like your worst project/idea ever. No one, but no one, warns you – least of all your own mother, who seems to genuinely believe herself when she says she forgot all the pain because you were worth it.

OK, so there were some indications that it might not be a party.

Once or twice during your pregnancy people mentioned the word 'uncomfortable', which is code for: It hurts like hell. But the whole process of subdivision is like a bad practical joke. I don't suppose there are many women in labour who don't at some point say, 'It's no good, I can't do it' and, given the option, would pay a great deal of money – probably all the money they have – to pack up their things and go home and forget the whole damn business. Alas.

Women today have it relatively easy … Birthing plans – even maternity wards – are relatively new. As recently as the beginning of the twentieth century, most women gave birth attended by midwives at home. It involved a lot of towels, newspaper, and for some reason a kettle. Other women who had presumably been through a lot of labours themselves delivered the babies, only calling on a doctor if things got tricky, if indeed there was time. It wasn't until the 1920s that obstetrics and gynaecology became a medical specialty. So it looks like less than one hundred years ago pain relief in labour amounted to biting on a tea towel.

There is a recent trend for mothers to bring their own mothers into the labour room as one of their birthing buddies … which is exciting (at least from my point of view. Except I am such a beady-eyes I shall probably be really embarrassing, ask too many questions and demand to see the supervisor if my daughter doesn't get as much attention as she deserves. And I wouldn't want to be the anaesthetist who dawdles when my daughter is screaming out for an epidural. My own mother had to content herself with having her hair set and making a batch of marmalade to take her mind off me being in labour) if I'm lucky enough to be there. I only hope people have the sense not to put me in charge of filming the video.

Of course if you're really famous you can just go and buy a baby when you fancy a new one. Or bring one home from trips abroad like we would bring home a giant Toblerone.

THINGS MOTHERS ARE GOOD AT

* Holding your hair back when you're being sick.
* Being bossy.
* Chivvying – with that sing-songy voice they do when you're little to lull you into a false sense of security when you are about to have an injection/plaster ripped off/your first tooth extraction.
* Putting lipstick on without using a mirror.
* Coat holding.
* Cheering you at sports day, charity walks, and speech day.
* No one makes a bed like your mum. It's the way they turn the top down so you can't fall out.
* Confidence provider – even when the evidence to the contrary is staring her in the face, she thinks her children look stunningly gorgeous.
* Fairy kisses.
* Sticking up for you.
* Wearing slippers so much they wear out.
* Switching situations around so they're now your fault.
* Being a good judge of character – mums have a way of being able to tell which of your friends genuinely like you.
* Cooking without ever referring to a recipe.
* Squirrelling away free stuff from hotels, including the biscuits.
* Knowing what's in the fridge without looking.
* Knowing which socks belong to who.
* Putting dried-up biros back in the mug by the phone.
* Being able to tell if fish has gone off just by sniffing it.
* Making a fuss of you when you're ill – there is no one like your mum when you're ill, especially when you're really only a little bit poorly but would like a nice day off in front of the fire.
* Finding any chocolate in the house. Even in a power cut.

✿ Getting things out of proportion.

✿ Shopping for clothes and then not admitting to anyone, not even herself, how much she really spent. I have a friend who, when she's been clothes shopping, hangs the bags on the front-door knocker, goes in through the kitchen to greet her husband, and then sneaks the bags up the stairs so that he doesn't see them. Good idea, eh?

THINGS MOTHERS ARE RUBBISH AT

- Climbing trees.
- Getting the names of bands right. Or is that groups?
- Running. Whoever invented the mother's day race at sports day had a seriously good sense of humour.
- Dealing with spiders.
- Getting out of the front door in under two hours.
- Putting a bra on without having to twist it round.
- Fairgrounds. They trust no one and are counting the minutes till they can leave. If they could make them illegal, they would.
- Relaxing.
- Having fun. Mothers do not have fun – at all. They are physically incapable. They have minus zero ability to have fun.
- Sleeping in.
- Not stressing.
- Working out foreign currency rates.
- Playing board games. They try. But if anything goes on for longer than about half an hour they wander off to get a chicken in the oven, or get the vegetables on. They can't really be bothered.

A MOTHER'S WORK IS NEVER DONE

t doesn't take a genius to work out that motherhood is both the hardest and the worst-paid job in the world. You don't even get Christmas Day off. Actually, you *so* don't get Christmas Day off. You can't call in sick, and the job-share arrangement you have with your partner really sucks since he doesn't take fatherhood tasks to work, whereas mothers do. Working mothers have two lists on the go, the work one and the motherhood one, hence their to-do lists can involve anything from sorting fungal infections and ringing the piano teacher to rearrange next week's pick-up time, to booking driving tests for teenagers online. And then on top of that they have the work to-do list. Both somehow get done because otherwise you'd go stark raving mad – that and, worse, you'd run out of bin liners.

It's not that dads are lazy, more their job description is different.

Mother's work:

* Doctor's and dentist's appointments
* Verrucas
* Sports kit – if dads are left to do it they just tell their kids to do it, and so it doesn't happen

- Sewing on name tags
- Party bags – dads don't understand party bags
- Getting hot-water bottles for people who don't feel very well
- Worrying
- Getting into a state about things
- Getting up in the night and putting kids back to sleep in their own beds

Dad's work:

- Getting up in the night and bringing kids back to bed instead of staying with them until they fall asleep in their own beds
- Telling mothers not to be so silly
- Making those raspberry noises with their cheeks at babies
- Fooling around and making children giggle while Mum gets the tea on
- Mending toys
- Bathtime

❧ Making sandcastles (this being the single most helpful thing a dad can do, leaving Mum free to soak up the sun or read *Grazia*)
❧ Getting the kids from under her feet because if he doesn't she might murder one of them

Somehow it works. And the reason it works is because mums are seriously clever. They must be clever, because despite making it look like all they think about is their family's happiness and never their own, mums actually get their own way 99 per cent of the time. This is an art mothers pick up from their own mother. Mums also manage to give out giant-sized dollops of guilt to anyone who dares to find them out. Again, a brilliant trick.

No one would deny that motherhood is seriously hard work; if you're not cleaning up bodily fluids and de-licing hair, then you're arranging play dates, which involves being very sociable with mothers you have nothing in common with – give me mopping up bodily fluids any day of the week.

It's not just the physical slog of it; motherhood simply clogs up your head, jams it full of things you need to remember: the judo kit, half-term dates, booking swimming lessons early enough to get the good instructor not the lousy one, as well as answering all the letters that come home from school.

Then, after eighteen years of it all, when you have a really bad-hair life and your house needs 'refreshing' (which is code for: Your kids have annihilated it), your youngest leaves home and hands you your P45 without so much as a redundancy package, consigning you to gardening leave for the foreseeable future when you don't much like gardening.

Whatever way you look at it, motherhood is a lousy job. So it's just as well that all mothers think of motherhood not as a job but more as a calling. God in his wisdom wired mothers in such a way as to not mind.

Mums have more to do at any one time than is strictly speaking possible, while constantly being interrupted. You start the ironing and get called away to talk to a friend who is going through a bitter divorce; you start helping one child with their spelling test and the other one needs tea before gymnastics … Mothers have come up with a solution to this problem of being constantly interrupted – it's called 'multi-tasking'. Every single thing mums do involves multi-tasking. Let's be honest, if they could multi-task while having sex, they would. Unfortunately, they're so busy multi-tasking that they never get around to having sex. Nor do they ever get around to sorting anything out, so mums spend a stupid amount of time looking for their glasses/that jar of paprika/their keys in their handbag …

In many ways mums are their own worst enemies. They have an astonishingly long list of things that they think are essential but other people are oblivious to; things like turning mattresses and rinsing swing bins. Worse, mothers decide that these things have to be done *now*.

In practice, every mother does things differently to her own mother, and inevitably gets some things right that her mother got wrong, and gets other things wrong that she got right. If we feel that as kids we were short-changed in the love-and-affection department by our own mothers, then chances are we will shower our own children with all the love and affection they can handle – resulting most likely in spoilt brats. If, on the other hand, we think we were allowed to get away with murder by our own mothers, then we turn into Norland Nannies without the uniform and end up with … children who wouldn't say boo to a goose. And so the cycle of motherhood goes on. The only difference now is that there are dozens of books and Channel 4 series to confuse us even more.

Not only is motherhood the hardest work imaginable, it's impossible to get it right. Unlike work-work, you can't measure good motherhood in targets or bonuses, there is no annual staff review or training programme. Basically, we all do our best.

Mums do the dirty work

Crucially you only get one mum, and she loves you unconditionally, irrespective of how many grade-A stars or detentions you accumulate. She would walk to the ends of the earth for you. If push came to shove she'd skip *EastEnders* for you. Just the once. She might even give you her last Malteser. Mothers will do anything for their children. And guess what: children work this out at a very early age.

Your children will dump everything on you for as long as you let them. Even when they've left home, they still call you up to problem-solve for them, or just to have a moan. My children save all the worst tasks for me. They know I am a sucker for punishment. The two of them have filled my life up with all sorts of tedious shit, like cashing in book tokens given to them on their birthdays by well-meaning relatives so that they can buy something more interesting. I recently had to cash in a Monsoon voucher that one of them had been given because they don't like Monsoon clothes. Well, neither do I much, but it now sits in my purse gathering dust and fraying at the edges.

The other day Ellen, my youngest – now 19, called me at work. 'Are you all right?' I said, wondering what domestic crisis I would have to attend to. 'Well, no, I'm not all right actually,' she said. My heart skipped a beat, I mentally already had her on a life support. 'You've put my best white bra in the machine and I specifically left it in the hand-wash pile. It's ruined – the padding's gone all lumpy. It's your fault.' Pause. As in: What are you going to do about it? 'OK, well, I didn't think I did …' 'Well, you obviously thought wrong, because I have my bra in my hand and it's ruined. Why can't you do any washing properly?' Rationally, she was being a little madam, but guess what: I raced into H&M on the way home to get her a new one, making me late and tired and fed up. She wasn't even that grateful. Why would she be? We are there to serve. Selflessly, tirelessly, silently, we are there to serve. Whether it's taking something back to Topshop that they've worn and decided they don't like after all, or booking train tickets, or writing their Geography project for them, or applying for jobs, opening bank accounts, or keeping them well stocked in tampons, we are the best and the cheapest backup service in the world.

The worst thing they can dump on you is worry. 'I'm worried about …' is where most of the trouble sentences start. Anything that your child describes as a worry becomes your worry. It's risen straight to the top of the worry pile – which is no mean feat – and you can't sleep or rest until you have done something about it. The trouble is, you put your own life on hold to sort it out, spending an entire morning emailing the headmistress or getting all steamed up about someone who has been unkind to them in the dinner queue, but by the time you report back with a solution they have *so* moved on to something else. You are the last to know.

Lifetime of servitude

The size of the workload when it first happens to you comes as a massive shock. You thought you had been busy at work; somehow you persuade yourself that, when the baby is born, you might have a bit of time to yourself. I remember saying to my husband that I might take an MA or retrain as a teacher while I was on maternity leave, or write a novel. Oh. My. God. The moment it happens you realise what you have signed up for is a life of servitude. Me-time is a thing of the past. Thirty seconds in the bathroom on your own, max.

You're flying solo. After that night in the ward when the nurses took pity on you and helped you change your first nappy when you couldn't really stand up straight or sit down, you discover that your life is defined not by what you want to do but what has to be done first. Even though you have been through the labour from hell – in my case a caesarean, which I swear must be similar to a hysterectomy (and women used to get about three months off work for that) – people assume that, now you're a mother, you will put your own medical emergency on hold.

I was a pitiful sight, trying to inch my way up and out of the bed to get to baby in the middle of the night. By day five or six I could manage a shuffle down the ward to the other non-caesarean mums, thinking that my predicament would be greeted with horror – only to find that everyone was in the same state, stitched-up front-bottoms being evidently as debilitating as full-on surgery. We all shuffled about the ward, pushing baby in our plastic wheelie see-through cots, looking like lardy war veterans.

The biggest shock was the night shift. As a novice nappy-changer, there were nights when I had to change baby's bed sheets and nightie three times to deal with leakages. I couldn't even breastfeed properly: my boobs were so big that poor baby kept falling off the nipple like someone sliding off a bouncy castle. God, I was in a state.

The workload doesn't improve once you get baby home. The hell of bringing baby home for the first few weeks can be summed up by the contents of a supermarket trolley I saw recently. The mum pushing it had baby in a sling, and among the mountain of baby stuff – nappies, nappy sacks, Sudocrem, SMA milk, cotton wool – there was only one non-baby item: a large bottle of vodka.

I remember bringing baby number one home and thinking, Well, I'll give this a go for a couple of weeks, but if I can't do it I'm going to hand her in to the authorities and I can just go and visit occasionally. The sheer and utter and total and completely unbelievable responsibility and hard work of it all hit me like a juggernaut when I was busy looking the other way, preoccupied with baby vests with bunnies on and gorgeous John Lewis baby towels and lemon changing mats and matching woolly booties and hats.

Being a full-time round-the-clock bodyguard with no relief shift or reliable backup, not to mention being their only source of food, comes at a price: your sanity. Almost as bad, despite having given birth to a baby you still look fat, you cry a lot, the hormonal roller coaster has sent you into bonkers land, and I for one needed my mother to sit me down and give me a good talking-to.

Looking in the mirror one afternoon when baby was a few months old and everyone else was going about their daily business, I realised that it had been nearly a week since I had worn anything but baggy jogging shorts and the kind of slippers ugly enough to peg out washing in. This would be fine were it not for the fact your partner is a little distraught at the prospect of spending the rest of his life with someone who looks like she has seriously let herself go. Not least because, if he were to tell her so, he would risk an electric-carving-knife-related incident in the night, or a slower death by rat poison. In this instance, the person who has to tell you that you are seriously letting yourself go is your own mother. This is part of her job description. Plus it's a whole lot better than your mother-in-law telling you.

Mothering small babies is easily the hardest work I have ever done. No, you can't sleep in. No, you can't go to the loo without taking baby too, and even then she might roll over and out of the door or die in a pool of her own sick, or choke on baby buds or ... And no, you can't get in the bath, and no, you can't fall asleep unless she does. And hey, guess what? She doesn't really seem to like sleep a whole lot.

Midwives and health visitors would tell me to let standards drop around the house, to chill out. So what if the washing needs doing or the house is ankle-deep in baby debris, they'd say. And some mothers seemed to adapt well to this and live like total slovens. Sadly, for someone like me, with control and tidiness issues, it was my worst nightmare all day every day: never ever catching up with the washing, or the hoovering, or just generally being able to live somewhere that didn't look as though a bomb had hit it. I nearly went insane with it all. But guess who saved the day and my sanity? My own mother. If it hadn't been for her ability to pick up baby, wind her (seemed to be my mother's obsession), take baby off my hands for an hour at a time, I would have gone stark raving mad. Although some people might say I *did* go stark raving mad.

My relationship with my own mother changed utterly when I myself gave birth. Overnight, I sort of got it. Before I was a mother myself, although I loved her very much, I thought she was a bit of a pain in the neck. Even when I was pregnant there was a little bit of me that didn't really get why she was so excited at the prospect of a grandchild. What's it got to do with her? I thought. It's my baby. But the moment she came into the maternity ward to see me, I hugged her and realised instantly, profoundly, how much she had loved me all those years, and how utterly mind-blowing that love is.

Well, that and the fact that, frankly, my mother was the only one who really knew what to do when we got baby home. My husband and I were floundering, trying to get a wriggling baby into anything other than a nightie, but Mum knew just what to do. I realised that in so many ways my mother was the one who had taught me all the important bits in life. Not how to do well at a job interview, not how to make a speech or do mental arithmetic. No, she taught me the stuff that matters: how to deal with nappy rash, how to get tea on the table within twenty minutes of walking in the door, how to cut an unsliced loaf and spread it with butter straight from the fridge, and how to be a black-belt gravy maker. Most importantly, she taught me how to be a mother. These are the things that count.

Better still, my mother sorted stuff. She set up a nappy-changing station in the living room so that I didn't have to climb all the stairs to the nursery; she soothed baby to sleep; she cooked me food, boiling chickens and chopping up bits of apple; she brought me hot-water bottles and tucked me in when I needed sleep. She was an absolutely brilliant mother. She lived for it, nothing else mattered to her.

It's only when you become a mother yourself that you realise just how brilliant your own mother is. I suspect that zillions of new mothers realise in one fell swoop how valuable, how utterly fabulous your own mother is when you become a mother. OK, so she would insist on putting baby into a hideous jade cardigan that her sister had made, and she would insist on leaving baby out in the fresh air when you considered it far too cold, and her idea of healthy first solids was a sugar-infested rusk, and if you hadn't been careful she would have got her hooked on a dummy ... But hey, we're splitting hairs.

Wired for Trouble

Once you're a mother, peace and quiet is a thing of the past. It's gone. Get over it. Even when they're eighteen you will be poised to leap into action if they need you. And there will be (many) times when you realise at three in the morning that they are still not home and start calling all the local A&E departments before realising they're sleeping over at a friend's house. When you hear a baby cry, even if it's not yours, you will hear it. You are now wired for trouble.

The whole point about motherhood is that it takes over your life. If it doesn't, you can't call yourself a proper, fully fledged, card-carrying mother. Mothers who have time for manicures, who blow dry the back of their hair as well as the front, or manage to fit in an afternoon nap are either royalty or bad mothers. Good mothers look like shit, except for those rare times they really make an effort. Real mothers are permanently hoarse and out of breath from yelling commands up the stairs.

Luckily, there are things that keep mothers going ...

THINGS THAT KEEP MOTHERS GOING

- Paintings that our children draw of us holding hands
- The odd gorgeous hug
- The smell of newly bathed infants
- Their favourite bedtime story
- Fairy kisses
- Retail therapy
- Dry white wine
- *Strictly*

To mummy
You are cuddly
You can make beautiful food I
Love You more than ny thing in the world. I Love You from Siena
X X X

Sometimes, however, mothers are their own worst enemies, discarding as too politically incorrect devices that their own mothers swore by. Like the playpen. Bring them back! we say – as long as we don't tell Amnesty International, this one is a winner.

THE THINGS MOTHERS SAY

If all your friends jumped off a bridge, would you?

That's neither funny nor clever.

Do you need the loo before we go?

Just in case.

It will come in handy.

I shan't tell you again.

It'll end in tears.

No one's looking at you.

Now you're just showing off.

Put your shoulders back.

Every cloud has a silver lining. [After that boyfriend she hated just dumped you.]

I'm doing this for your own good.

You don't need to know the reason why.

Don't try to pull the wool over my eyes.

You must think I was born yesterday.

I could murder a nice cup of tea.

Not in these shoes, I can't.

If you can't be good, be careful.

I can feel a draught.

No means no.

Go careful.

The fresh air will do you good.

You don't know where that's been.

We'll see.

Play nicely.

Because I said so.

Don't make me count to ten.

Don't be cheeky.

Stop answering back.

'I want' doesn't get.

Will someone get these children out from under my feet?

You'll thank me.

Hurry up.

Get up. NOW.

I thought you would have phoned earlier.

Don't make me come down there and show you.

Not what I'd call clean.

Have you sent off your thank you cards yet?

Clean costs nothing.

Don't eat with your mouth full.

Use a hanky.

Weren't you supposed to hand that in last week?

Give it here, I'll do it.

What's the magic word?

Did you say thank you?

Shall we play a game?

I liked yours the best.

Don't run before you can walk.

You'll understand one day.

It wasn't like that in my day.

Has anyone seen my glasses?
[Answer: They're on your head.]

Have you noticed something different about me?
[To husband after a haircut.]

I wouldn't give it houseroom.

I'm exhausted. [Constantly.]

What did your last slave die of?

Close the door, you weren't born in a barn.

I can't hear myself think.

It will all end in tears.

It will all come out in the wash.

Who's 'she'? The cat's mother?

Don't make that face. If the wind
changes you'll stay like that.

You'll catch your death in that.

You don't get a pudding if you don't eat your mains.

Did you keep the receipt?

You don't know you're born.

I can put my hand right on it.

You haven't looked properly.

You haven't done it properly.

Anything with the word 'properly' in the sentence.

Wash it and put it away.

Don't get peas above sticks. [Any cocky behaviour.]

Do I look as old as her?

Do I look as fat as her?

What a lovely service.

Yes, but have you checked?

THINGS MOTHERS DON'T SAY

Have it your way.

I'll fall in with everyone else.

Why don't I treat you to a tattoo!

Make that a double.

Why not have a party while Dad and I are away?

I'll leave it entirely up to you.

Here's my credit card and pin number.

Don't worry about cleaning up your mess.

The vodka's in the kitchen cupboard.

I'd rather you didn't come home for Christmas.

Stay-at-home mums

Stay-at-home mums have copped for a fair amount of insults – mostly, it has to be said, from working mothers. Hence people are frightened to ask whether they work or not, so they say 'Do you work outside the home?' for fear of having their heads ripped off by angry stay-at-home mums who feel undervalued by people saying, 'It must be nice not to have anything to do all day,' or 'Your house must be spotless with so much time to clean,' or, worst of all, 'Can you pick up my child from school, since you're not doing anything?' Stay-at-home mums silently reply that they wish they had an hour-long lunch break, or sick leave, or a company car, or a grievance procedure …

Working mums

Career mothers are relatively new. Up until the sixties, if Mum did contribute to the family purse it was as an Avon Lady – one of a handful of respectable forms of income. As recently as the fifties most women spent on average 78.9 hours per week tending the children or the house. With no washing machine, vacuum cleaner or microwave, most mothering duties involved hard graft and were time consuming. Back then, mums still laundered using a washboard, and having a kettle was considered the height of sophistication.

What is shocking is that now, with most mums in employment, they still spend nigh on 78.9 hours engaged in family- or home-related tasks. The only difference is that they have a job too. Mind you, our obsession with cleanliness doesn't help. Back in the fifties the kids had a bath and washed their hair once a week, people changed their sheets very infrequently and basically everyone ponged a bit … Get over it!

Quality time

Once mothers started going out to work someone had to invent something that sugared the pill and kept the guilt at bay. Enter quality time. Trouble is, children don't really get quality time. As a working mother you break your neck to get home early to pick them up from school for the all-important quality time, yet the harder you try, the worse it gets, and you resort to asking inane questions like 'How was school today?' 'What did you do in school?' 'What did you have for lunch?' Basically, children only tell you stuff when they want to, so questions achieve nothing. Hence TV on a tray in front of *Neighbours* – you may be watching TV, but you're together, and that's all that matters.

But here's the miracle: despite all the work involved, for most of us being a mother is the single best thing in life, the one thing you'd do again and again and again if you could. It's probably just as well that God stops women having more babies with the menopause, otherwise I for one would have gone back for more.

THE RULE of THREE

n email which circulated on the net a while ago described how standards inevitably slip by the time number three comes along:

Your clothes
✿ **First baby:** You begin wearing maternity clothes as soon as your pregnancy is confirmed.
✿ **Second baby:** You wear your regular clothes for as long as possible.
✿ **Third baby:** Your maternity clothes ARE your regular clothes.

Preparing for the birth
✿ **First baby:** You practise your breathing religiously.
✿ **Second baby:** You don't bother because you remember that last time breathing didn't do a fat lot to help.
✿ **Third baby:** You ask for an epidural on arrival at hospital.

Getting ready for baby
✿ **First baby:** You pre-wash newborn's clothes, colour-coordinate them, and fold them neatly in the baby's room.
✿ **Second baby:** You check to make sure that the clothes are clean and discard only the ones with the darkest stains.

✿ **Third baby:** Boys can wear pink, can't they?

Worries

✿ **First baby:** At the first sign of distress – a whimper, a frown – you pick up the baby.

✿ **Second baby:** You pick the baby up when her wails threaten to wake your firstborn.

✿ **Third baby:** You teach your three-year-old how to rewind the mechanical swing.

Dummy

✿ **First baby:** If the dummy falls on the floor, you put it away until you can go home and wash and boil it.

✿ **Second baby:** When the dummy falls on the floor, you squirt it off with some juice from the baby's bottle.

✿ **Third baby:** You wipe it off on your shirt and pop it back in.

Nappies

✿ **First baby:** You change your baby's nappies every hour, whether they need it or not.

✿ **Second baby:** You change their nappy every two to three hours, if needed.

✿ **Third baby:** You try to change their nappy before others start to complain about the smell or you see it sagging to their knees.

Activities

✿ **First baby:** You take your infant to baby gymnastics, mother-and-baby swimming sessions and baby story hour.

✿ **Second baby:** You take your infant to baby gymnastics.

✿ **Third baby:** You take your infant to the supermarket and the dry cleaner.

Going out

❀ **First baby:** The first time you leave your baby with a sitter, you call home five times.

❀ **Second baby:** Just before you walk out the door, you remember to leave a number where you can be reached.

❀ **Third baby:** You leave instructions for the sitter to call only if she sees blood.

At home

❀ **First baby:** You spend a good bit of every day just gazing at the baby.

❀ **Second baby:** You spend a bit of every day watching to be sure your older child isn't squeezing, poking, or hitting the baby.

❀ **Third baby:** You spend a little bit of every day hiding from the children.

Swallowing coins (a favourite trick)

❀ **First child:** When first child swallows a coin, you rush them to the hospital and demand X-rays.

❀ **Second child:** When second child swallows a coin, you carefully watch for the coin to pass.

❀ **Third child:** When third child swallows a coin you deduct it from his pocket money!

Interestingly, third-borns turn out surprisingly well. Perhaps mothers, when distracted, might be a whole lot easier to live with.

LOOK AT ME WHEN I'M TALKING TO YOU

Children are naughty and they're inquisitive, which would be fine if mothers didn't have a lot on their plate. The result is that mothers become extremely bossy. Annoyingly, fathers often avoid this, and despite the fact that mothers resort to occasionally saying, 'Wait till your father gets home.' Once he does get home it's all been sorted; either that or he doesn't really see why making such a huge mess in the living room or leaving your broccoli untouched on your plate was such a big deal.

Disciplining, like so much of motherhood, has got harder than it was. Motherhood has changed beyond recognition over the space of three generations. In granny's day, unless you were very upper class, you had your children under your feet from morning till night (if you were very posh you farmed them out and working-class mothers took them in). Children everywhere, whatever their class, were seen and not heard. They knew their place, and most of them had to make do with amusing themselves.

Bizarrely, just as mothers started to go out to work, motherhood got harder and more hands-on – a double whammy. You go out to work, you feel guilty, and you come home to even more work. What this means is that there are some very tired, very bad-tempered mothers out there. I count myself among them.

Smacking is no longer an option, and biting is not a politically correct alternative. Our youngest had a habit of biting other children, which of course is very, very wrong. Worse, it was very, very difficult to deny because she left teethmarks.

I was always really rubbish at being naughty. Or, more accurately, very good at getting caught. When I was eleven we had a foreign exchange student staying with us who was thirteen and properly grown up and who wore miniskirts and make-up and knew about sex and everything. I had been told by my mother on no account ever to hitch-hike, but one evening the French girl persuaded me to give it a try. We were only going out for some fish and chips and a lurk about the park, like you do. I'd only had my thumb out for about thirty seconds when my parents' Ford Anglia drove past. Just my luck! The word grounded hadn't been invented then, but I think my mother sulked and barely spoke to me for weeks, which was much more effective.

Parental discipline is a tricky one. I have always admired mothers who can go to the supermarket and get their children to stop doing anything at all, or who only have to give their children a disapproving look for them to stop whatever naughtiness they might be up to. A look wouldn't even have been noticed by my two. We put Ellen in the cloakroom when she was naughty, but she was far too bright for it to work; it took her about two sessions to realise that the cloakroom had a sink and so turning both taps on full and putting the plug in would get her released immediately. There is nothing like an emergency needing a mop and bucket to head your mother's best-laid plans off at the pass. Ellen's other trick was putting everything down the loo:

keys, cotton wool, make-up, perfume, nappies … She thought this was the funniest thing ever. I should have retrained as a plumber.

The Naughty Step

Is fine until kids figure out that sitting on the step's not too bad. Besides, they know that Mum has got to get them off to school in five minutes anyway. The naughty step works when Mum has got all the time and patience in the world to keep you there until you can be good. *She never does have time.*

I'm Counting to Three

Oh dear. If only mothers could see themselves. It's so humiliating to watch a mother stretching out two and a half to three in multiples of ten. The reality is, it's about who is going to give in first: mother or child. And children have all the time in the world …

Words

Other weapons in mothers' armoury are words. The word of mass destruction that mothers use when they are angry with their children, the one that stops you in your tracks and makes you feel a bit sick is *disappointed*. I'm disappointed in you.

The word disappointed is such an Exocet, coming from your mother. If she uses the D word you know that your mother very badly wants you to take notice or change your behaviour.

Bribery

Most mothers resort to bribery. We've had it up to here, we can't hear ourselves think, they won't hurry up, and they've just trod mud all up the stairs. So we throw bribery at the problem in the shape of sweets, toys, trips to Alton Towers … Anything for some peace and quiet – or more likely being able to get on with what you need to do.

Educationally Sound Bribery

Some mothers go the star-chart route – encouraging their children to be good by meritocracy rather than straightforward bribery. This makes mothers feel both fragrant and educationally sound. Some mothers go so far as to laminate the star charts and stick them on the kitchen wall, although this suggests to me they need to get out more. Stars are earned by doing domestic tasks such as unloading the dishwasher, or cleaning out the gerbil, which is all very well. But for the charts to work they have to involve some meaningful bribery – in my experience a gold star loses its lustrous appeal after about Day 2, and most children will ignore it. For bribery to work, money must change hands. Get over it. Once they're teenagers, of course, you will be paying them to do the ironing and other household chores for you. They won't do it very quickly, or when you want them to, but it'll get stuff off your list and mean you don't just give them handouts. Everyone's (relatively) happy.

Don't Be Cheeky

This is what mothers say when they have run out of bribery/patience/can't be bothered to explain anything any more.

As a kid, you know you've won the battle when she uses this phrase.

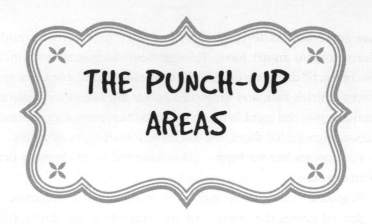

THE PUNCH-UP AREAS

Manners

Mothers who spend a lot of time disciplining their children when it comes to manners have well-behaved children. Pleases and thank yous are for good children. But the fact is, if your child likes playing with fire extinguishers or has found out how to start the car and reverse it down the drive, manners are a bit irrelevant.

Saying Sorry

One of the wonderful things about children is that they can only say sorry if they mean it. When they're made to say sorry, it comes out all wrong. If they spontaneously come up to you and say sorry it's genuine. Adults unfortunately learn the art of saying sorry when they don't mean it at all.

Tidiness

Anyone who has stepped on a piece of Lego with bare feet knows how maddening toys are when they're left sprawling all over the house. One of the huge advantages the middle class enjoy is a playroom. Somewhere to scoop it all up at the end of the day is a joy indeed.

Teenagers use tidiness as a weapon. No child wants a clean bedroom. No mother wants one fifth of her house to look like a landfill and be a toxic no-go area. Teenagers work out that they have some serious leverage here, and they have turned untidy bedrooms into an art form. Teenage boys' bedrooms have their own indescribable pong to go with the mess – a combination of wet towels, athlete's foot, and unwashed sports kit. Girls can create so many layers of nail varnish, empty vodka bottles, pants, leggings, and hideous high-heeled shoes that you could mount a geological dig.

First comes the warning – 'This weekend we're cleaning that room of yours.'

Response – daughter spends entire weekend out of the house.

Second comes the threat – 'If you don't do it, I'll throw it all away.'

Response – daughter buys a lock for door.

Third comes the blackmail – 'If you don't do it now, I will take x away from you.'

Daughter is now cornered. Deprivation of phone/Mum's taxi service/allowance would result in her being stranded in 'saddo' territory. Thus she is left with one option: to cave in and get on with it. Thus, for the first time since Daughter became a teen, Mum gets to see the contents of her room – which will contain any combination of the following:

✿ Mouldy food
✿ Old, dirty underwear
✿ Her boyfriend's old, dirty underwear
✿ A very bad poem written to the boyfriend before they got together
✿ A very angry letter written after she and the boyfriend split up
✿ Your things
✿ Her sister's things
✿ Confiscated items of clothing
✿ Someone else's pet

Dear Mum
We cleared the Kitchin
love
Ellen and Siena

- Damning school reports you've never seen
- Forged letters to the school saying you've read the school report which you've never seen
- Tattoo/body-piercing brochures
- Inappropriate underwear
- The £200 phone bill Dad paid without telling you
- Ticket stubs for night clubs
- Men's phone numbers
- Chocolate body paint
- A home 'vajazzling' kit
- Cigarettes

This will be both a bonding experience, a moment of catharsis and horribly illuminating – you have been warned. If you believe you should share everything with your daughter then step inside her domain. On the other hand, if you don't want to know she had an STD exam, told her Maths teacher to 'stick his compass up his arse', or flirted with the idea of a nipple-piercing, then perhaps it might be better to try and ignore the mess.

Sometimes ignorance is bliss.

ANNOYING THINGS MOTHERS DO

others do a lot of annoying things. That's because they're annoying. Whether it's saving things for best, invariably being right, or just being a complete nag, they are infuriating.

They often become annoying suddenly and with no warning. One minute your mother is the best person in the world, simply the only person who understands you, and then suddenly she is the most irritating person you've ever met. Like a really bad smell that wafts in through a car window, you go off her. Everything about her – the way she talks, the way she sits, even the way she breathes – is abhorrent to you. It may be that she asks you something stupid like, 'What are you thinking about?' or expresses disappointment in your exam results. Or you realise that she has been snooping on your Facebook page or talking to your teacher behind your back. Or she might just purse her lips into that pout that means she feels you've let her down.

At times like these, it's all you can do to stop yourself murdering her.

Worse still, mothers always have to occupy the moral high ground. They never admit that they are lazy good-for-nothings – which all mothers are, from time to time. They pretend they've made a strawberry tart from scratch when you know full well it has come out of a pack or kit or a jar. They assume no one will catch them out because when you were four you didn't know any different, but then you grow up and find shameful evidence of domestic shortcuts in the cupboard: gravy granules, no less; packs of shortcrust pastry; and tins of already shredded marmalade oranges pickled in e numbers to make into 'home-made' marmalade. Mothers have even been known to make soup out of a packet and call it home-made.

Sometimes mothers can be devilishly devious. OK, normally to achieve admirable ends, such as getting some food down a sick child, or getting vegetables into a vegetarian child who doesn't like vegetables. When my children went through their vegetarian phase I used to sneak chicken stock into whatever I could, or pretend I had made two gravies when I had not. So occasionally mothers' devious tendencies are forgivable, but even with the really bad stuff mothers rarely admit they're guilty as charged. Like when Mum 'borrows' your things, or your father's. You know she's nicked your favourite shampoo; Dad knows she used his razor to shave her legs; you know she didn't wash it by hand; and you both know she's only washing up so that she can pick on the leftovers … But that won't stop mums from hiding behind a smokescreen of being Little Miss Innocent. In other words, mothers always have to be right.

Mothers also tend to have double standards. It's a case of 'Do as I say, not as I do' – there's one rule for her and one rule for everyone else. If she leaves the immersion on it's OK, if anyone else does there'll be hell to pay. Her own mess is OK, but everyone else's is abhorrent to her and must be cleared up pronto. While it's fine for her and Dad to get sozzled down the local and then stumble back through someone else's garden, if her daughter tries to go clubbing she will undoubtedly draw her attention to the horror stories on the news – tales of death/GBH/abduction/kidnap – and plead 'Imagine how her poor mother feels' before slipping out the front door and announcing she'll be back after last orders.

Mothers are a law unto themselves.

other annoying things mums do
(no room to cover them all, obviously)

❀ They have a problem with bins. They refuse to use a bin – as in a proper kitchen bin – preferring to use plastic supermarket carrier bags that hang on the kitchen door knob. Irritating.

❀ One way or another they make rubbish their business. They can't just chuck stuff away, they have to sort it, sift it, move it, label it … And ultimately they want to know what everyone else in the house has done with their rubbish too. They become rubbish bores.

❀ They have a way of making you feel guilty. All the time. 'Never mind, forget it' is most mothers' favourite line. Mothers have the ability to induce elephant-sized guilt with the smallest change in tone – particularly if you phone them less frequently than they would like, which is universally the case.

❀ Some mothers who had their children relatively young claim they 'missed out on their youth', which they cite as a reason to go clubbing with their daughter, say on her eighteenth, along with all her friends – who call themselves the 'crazy crew' (cringe). No, any mother who joins in clubbing or pub crawling is very annoying indeed.

❀ Whatever it is they want doing, they want it doing now.

❀ They busy themselves with pointless activities like lining kitchen drawers with gingham sticky-backed plastic.

❀ They clean before the cleaner comes.

- They spot dirt where dirt is invisible; on a bad day they floss behind radiators.

- For mothers hovering is a necessity not a personal lifestyle choice.

- Selective invisibility – your clutter gets put in piles – hers is allowed to sprawl all over the house.

- They need to get out more.

- They send you to the supermarket and put 'nice tomatoes' on the list. Like, unless she said that, we'd buy horrible ones. Actually, I think my father might have bought horrible ones just to ensure he wouldn't be sent again, but that's by the by.

- They like to know about the man situation in your life. If you mention a guy, he's instantly a prospective son-in-law.

- They want to make sure you've had your breakfast. You're thirty-two.

- They ask pointless questions like 'What did you have for lunch?' when you live four hundred miles away.

- They have an opinion on everything, from what food you should eat, to who you should spend your time with, to what you should do for a career. We know it's always done with the best intentions, but sometimes that's the most frustrating part – trumped only by the ultimate annoyance of finding out she was right all along.

- Their obsession with waste. They won't waste a scrap of food, which means that if you're not careful they'll feed you a lifetime of leftovers, with scraps of food in the carry-forward column the whole time – even though the original meal was sometime in 1985.

❀ Nagging is irritating is enough in itself, but what's worse is that it generally causes an argument about nagging, which then leads to another argument about what happens if she doesn't nag, bringing up even more nagging-related disputes from the past.

❀ Mothers are incapable of delegating without checking on whether you've done it, asking how you are getting on with that task she gave you.

❀ She thinks she's the only person who ever does anything. If she doesn't do it, no one else will. No, they won't – because no one else gives a stuff whether it's done or not.

❀ They're never satisfied.

❀ They suffer from an addiction to floral patterns.

❀ They will gush on about lilacs, and blossom on trees and the birds singing. Like that's interesting.

❀ They move everything. Apparently, everything being tidy is more important than you being able to find anything (although this can be embarrassing when you realise you have moved it yourself). For some reason they think they know best where everything should be kept/moved/stored. They have tragic systems that are to be obeyed by the whole household: one for bags with things to go back, one for things to go to the tip, one for the charity shop, one for recycling, one for please sort this out, one for take this upstairs, one for wash this up or there'll be trouble … In other words, everything – absolutely everything – in the house has her stamp on it. One way or another it has been 'processed' by she who must be obeyed. Stuff can't just lie about, it has to be tidied. Shoes must be put in pairs under chairs, washing is put in piles, socks are paired, glasses are put in rows according to their type, magazines and newspapers are tidied into piles or put in the recycling the moment they are out of date. NO SIGN OF HUMAN HABITATION WHATSOEVER MAY BE VISIBLE TO THE NAKED EYE.

✿ They are terrible at washing. Now I know this is a contradiction in terms in that mothers probably do most of the washing in any given household, but here's the problem: they always do it in a rush. They never read care labels; for one thing, it might involve finding their reading specs and they have not yet resorted to the David Dickinson look of specs on chains. They can't be bothered to learn about the different cycles the machine does. They choose one wash the first time they use it (in our house it stays on E) then whatever it is, whatever the circumstances, any washing always goes on that cycle.

✿ They wash everything. What is it with mothers? They can't let washing pile up for even a day; it has to be washed the moment it's taken off. For some reason if the washing piles up, mothers turn into jibbering wrecks. They just can't handle it, their lives fall apart and they can't operate as civilised human beings, resorting instead to shouting and screaming like a toddler.

✿ Equally, if the ironing piles up for more than a couple of days mothers have to be taken away to institutions or a happier place. They simply go insane.

❀ They are their own worst enemies when it comes to ironing. Mothers like everything ironed. Even non-iron or scrunch shirts that when you iron them go all baggy and you have to throw them away. They iron serviettes (sorry, napkins), sheets, pillow cases, towels, even tea towels. Like anyone else gives a shit. Some mothers even iron underwear. Trouble is, they can't be bothered to change the setting on the iron so they burn underwear too. Just so that it scratches when you wear it.

❀ They're a law unto themselves. They complain about their weight then eat an entire Thornton's Continental box in one sitting, but then when they are down to the last one or just the horrible soft-centred ones they say, 'Take this chocolate away from me,' or 'Don't let me have any more.' They pick while they're cooking. Why do you think they normally do the cooking? They pick and pick and then they sit down and tell you they're not very hungry, or only eat very little.

❀ Not ordering a pudding because she couldn't possibly, and then when you do she stops the waiter and says, 'Oh, by the way, can you bring two spoons.' Get your own pudding.

❀ They're illogical. 'There's plenty of time for all that' being one of the most frustrating examples. What, so you shouldn't go to a party with your mates because you need to save up the fun for later in life? Eh?

❀ They have control issues, hence they will write endless notes everywhere. On your bed, on your door …

❀ … On the fridge. *Please remember to send a card to your Aunty Dorothy. Please do not leave shoes by the front door. Please put all recycling rubbish in the right bin …* They write notes for you to put 'out' when you have put the immersion on. And no one pays any attention to their notes, which makes them mad as hell. But some mothers go over the top on notes. Less of the notes, please.

❀ They make you endure Mum TV. When Mum has the remote, there are but five options:

1. The Soaps
2. The Soaps
3. The Soaps
4. The Soaps
5. *Midsomer Murders* (for variety … but only if it doesn't clash with The Soaps)

❀ They politely 'remind' you how to do complex tasks like … stopping at a stop sign, locking a door, salting food, etc.

❀ They have the same bedtime they had when they were six.

❀ As the homeowner, they consider they have the right to enter any room at any given time. A locked door is seen as an admission that you have something to hide, but it also means that mums can be far, far too lax with their nudity.

❀ They're two-faced. My mother can be as nice as pie to the outside world. Charm itself, as chatty and as lovely as you like with someone in the street, normally another woman … Then the moment you both walk away, she says, 'I can't stand that woman.' She's entirely unpredictable; one minute she is charm itself, the next you wouldn't want to stand near her if she was carrying a knife – and it can change in a flash.

❀ Mums have an ability to erase their own teenage years from their life history while admonishing the daughter who dares to get drunk/smoke cigarettes/stay out late with boyfriend/wag off school. A fairly normal childhood becomes transformed into *Anne of Green Gables* and suddenly she has the past of a *Blue Peter* presenter … when the truth is she might have had Anthea's haircut but that didn't stop her having her Richard Bacon moments. Nevertheless she wants you to behave, to avoid making her mistakes. So she airbrushes out the seventeenth birthday when she ate six hash cakes and ended up in A&E. Gone is the episode when 'sexy Jeff' had to jump out of her bedroom window cos Nan came home early. Because if she did all that, then you might too, and when you do any of the above you will of course DIE.

❀ In short, mothers are very annoying indeed.

Wanna-be-best-friend mums

As any teenager knows, there are a handful of things mothers should never be:

1. Intentionally funny. We can laugh *at* you, but very rarely *with* you.
2. Sexy. Just yuck!
3. Your best friend.

Mums who want to be your friend are very dangerous. Some normal mums play this card at 'boyfriend' age, thinking that they can get some advice under the radar. To save time, a few mum questions can be debunked as follows:

1. 'You've been out with Nick a lot lately then?' – Translation: I'm too young to be a grandma.
2. 'That friend of yours, Emma, she's got a bit of a reputation, hasn't she?' – Translation: Emma's a slag. Stay away from her.
3. 'I hear there's some sort of a house party going on at David's.' – Translation: If you go, I'll know, and I will find out everything you do there.
4. 'I've heard your school discos are a bit wild.' – Translation: If you're sick, me and your dad aren't coming to pick you up.

Fine, but some poor souls have mums who truly WANT to be best friends, without a hidden agenda to check that you're not having sex/taking drugs/drinking. Mums who genuinely believe that the best style of parenting is one in which you can openly discuss sexual positions and the latest range at Ann Summers. This mothering style should come with a government health warning. It's just plain creepy.

Me and Mummy having lunch
Lucy McGregor aged 9.

YOU LOVE THEM MORE THAN YOU LOVE ME

A s a child you can't understand why a capable woman like your mother, who is clever enough to know several uses for bicarbonate of soda and can cut unsliced bread properly, could have let this happen. She informs you she is having another baby. As a toddler you may not grasp the full horror of the implications, but nevertheless you feel a sense of shock and disapproval.

You thought you were special enough for her not to need another child and you never thought she'd have any desire for the physical act that led to it. If the term 'an accident' was used to describe her pregnancy by aunts tipsy on sherry then this also stopped you in your tracks. Accident implies something happens a lot. Worst of all, you will have experienced a profound concern that you will never get your own way ever again. Which proves to be entirely accurate.

Once mothers have owned up to having another baby on the way they mount a full-on campaign to persuade you that you will enjoy having a lovely new sister or brother to play with – as if some blob of a baby is going to be able to play with your wish-for-a-pony set or sit still while you are cutting her hair. No. Sometimes mothers are so naive.

When our second baby arrived, our first refused to look in the cot. Despite accepting the bribe of presents 'from the new baby', eldest smelt trouble. Suddenly, here was tangible proof that she was going to be pushed out of the way. One mum who tried to win her daughter over by describing the new baby sister as a 'gift', was told, 'I'd rather have a My Little Pony.'

As an only child myself, nothing could have prepared me for the difficulties of sibling rivalry.

Typically, first children are sensitive souls. They've not had to push and shove, they've had their mothers all to themselves, and with luck grandparents, childminders or nannies too. They don't really get sharing. They've had all they want of you and then some. You have had time to read them stories after lunch, take them on day trips to the zoo, and their lives are carefree. Then along comes number two and it's hard not to be sympathetic when considering the effect it has on the eldest. Worse still, second-borns instinctively shove their elder siblings off the radar to make sure that there is only one person who is going to dominate their mother's time – them. All of which makes fairness totally impossible. One sibling will be the easy one who goes to sleep with no bother and makes few demands, while the other (or others) are troublemakers who decide that sleep is for sissies and constantly clamour for attention. Subconsciously, siblings seem to work all this out. Eldest children may be the quiet ones, but often it's simply because they've adopted a different strategy, having figured out how to play their mother for optimum results. Being the 'good' one, the one that doesn't make a fuss, might not get you the immediate reward that the naughty younger child gets, but as soon as there is something big at stake they will be the winner every time. So they don't make a great big song and dance about whether they sit in the front or the back of the car, they offer to help after meals once in a while, and they sit on their growing stash of brownie points. The younger one probably thinks they're daft, until the day there is something significant at stake – like who's getting the top bunk on a fortnight's holiday

– and the quiet one pipes up and reminds everyone that they don't normally ask for anything but on this occasion they would appreciate sleeping on the top bunk. Job done.

Second children come from a different gene pool. Our baby number two was quite a handful. She was the kind of baby that could sense when older sister had put the finishing touches to her princess painting, at which point youngest would toddle over and basically just sit on it. Or she'd wait until Mummy had bathed her, talced her, and put her to bed promising some quality time for big sister, only to commence bouts of cot screaming at five-minute intervals thereafter.

There is a photo of my two which captures their difference in character, defined I'm sure as much by their birth order as anything genetic: they're both dressed for pony trekking. Big sister is in the foreground wearing a hand-knitted jumper my mother made (quite badly) for her, looking shy and pigeon-toed and awkward; behind her stands her little sister, steadfast, steely, unfazed, and looking like she'd give Mike Tyson a run for his money.

Short of a straitjacket or a padded cell – to put one sibling in while I looked after the other – I'm not sure how as a mother I could have shared out my attention more fairly. Like all mothers, I tried the taking turns option and, most importantly, counting out to the penny how much was spent on each sister at Christmas and birthdays to make sure it was equal. We have a family birthday tradition which involves balloons being tied on the stair banisters on birthday mornings. One day baby sister decided to count her balloons and discovered she had two less than her sister had had on her birthday. Forget teaching arithmetic with coloured counters – they learn fast when it involves sibling rivalry.

When our two were small we went to Disneyland. One starlit night, after the pointless but time-consuming street carnival, eldest and I sat gazing at the stars by a wishing well. 'Oh, how lovely – perhaps you should make a wish,' I told her. 'What would I wish for?' she replied. 'Well, to always be happy,' I said, cunningly avoiding any pony- or dog-related wishes. 'I could never do that,' she said. 'Why not?' answer …'Ellen's alive.'

Not that being the youngest is all good. Some children see the order of conception as a race to be won and lost. I have a friend who refers to his little brother as the 'runner-up'. Younger children also have to cope with hand-me-down culture: by the time they get the hula hoop it's deeply out of fashion or a sign of geekdom; by the time they get Barbie she's going through the menopause; by the time they get the only decent bedroom in the house the bed has lost all its springs.

It's not as if smaller kids can get even. Once mothers have more than one child the only sensible approach is 'I DON'T CARE WHO DID IT' – which the guilty child sees as victory and the innocent child interprets as the ultimate treason. Most children will agree it's who DESERVED it that matters. OK, so they poured a bowl of Shreddies over their sister's head or pushed her over in a pile of fresh dog poo, but the whole thing was *her* fault.

Rule 1:
The turns with the control alternate
each day between Siena and Ellen.
Rule 2:
If you are not at home on your control day then it still counts as your
turn.
Rule 3:
If it is 1 person's turn with the control and they want to watch something on normal TV, but the other
Person wants to watch something on
SKY, then the person who's control
turn it is must move somewhere else
and viser verser.
Rule 4:
The person who's control turn it is
chooses what programme you watch
on whichever TV she chooses to

Watch, but rule 3 still applies.
Rule 5:
The persons who's turn it is with the
control's initial is on the calendar.
Rule 6:
The person who's turn it is with the
control gets to choose where they
sit.
Rule 7:
If you are band from the control for
any reason, rule 3 still applies
Rule 8:
The person who's turn it is with the
control, if they want to watch a
DVD or video, they gets to choose
which TV they use.

*Rule 6:
The initial of the person whose
turn it is with the control is on the
calendar.

Sign here if you agree with these
rules.

Control
Rule Booklet

The clever sibling never casts the first blow. Usually the oldest sibling just makes the younger ones as mad as hell, and having lit the touchpaper they retire to the moral high ground while the others get punished. It's called experience, and it's called having had your nose put out of joint big time. Clever siblings never hit back, because Mum always catches the second person. No wonder kids like to play the birth video of their siblings – but in reverse.

Luckily older children have some tools to get their own back. Take this example:

My brothers were two years apart and did a lot of stuff together. Once when the older one wasn't being particularly watched, he started writing on the walls. He was old enough to know better

because he wrote his name and all kind of things but at the end, he wrote DAVID DID THIS, which was my other brother's name … and who could not write at the time.

Nice one. I wonder if this boy is now a politician.

Clothes are a big trigger factor for sibling rivalry, especially with sibling girls. When the older one gets something nice, it almost always ends up in the younger one's wardrobe or drawer. As a mother you can immediately tell when this happens, because there is a lot of door slamming, stomping in and out of rooms, and ransacking the other one's room to find the missing item.

'That's mine!'

'I've only borrowed it.'

'I didn't say you could borrow it.'

'So what? You never wear it! You're too big anyhow!'

Then comes the chorus of 'MUM!'

Oh great, as a mother that means you have to referee. Referees never get it right. They can't please anyone any of the time, never mind all of the time.

Despite all this, some mothers inexplicably even go for the third child …

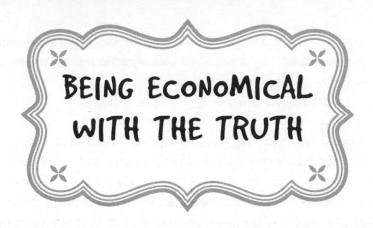

BEING ECONOMICAL WITH THE TRUTH

others are economical with the truth big time. They pretend that they're terrible at lying, and you believe them. But then, you would – because they're good at lying. How else would they be so adept at spotting when someone else is fibbing? It takes one to know one.

For some reason, mothers are allowed to tell great big whoppers and it's perfectly acceptable. Father Christmas, tooth fairies, gooseberry bushes, bogeymen who come to get naughty boys and girls ... Motherhood turns us into really good liars.

Some lies we tell are designed to spare our innocent darlings the ugly truth about the evil world they live in. Plus we can't cope with the emotional fallout that would ensue if the truth were told – not when *Corrie*'s about to start. When my children asked – as inevitably kids do – where meat comes from, I told them that meat came from dead animals. But what I didn't tell them was that humans actually kill the animals on purpose to eat them.

It's a mother's job to be economical with the truth.

Some lies that mothers tell

❀ We'll see. [This is code for: 'Not a chance in hell but I will deal with the fallout in stages or when I've poured myself a great big glass of wine.]

✿ Your father and I have decided. [I have decided.]

✿ I wouldn't dream of snooping round your things. [Whoops, I had better cover my tracks better next time.]

✿ Of course I haven't moved it. [I so have moved it, but I can't remember where the hell I've put it.]

✿ If you watch too much TV you'll get square eyes. [Get out into the fresh air, you lazy kids – I want to hoover in here.]

✿ If you don't clean your ears, potatoes will grow in them. [Well, that's just a bit bonkers, but apparently mothers do say it.]

✿ If you sulk like that your face will stick like it. [You're really getting on my nerves.]

✿ The pet dog/cat/guinea pig went to live on a farm. [They're in the back of the car because they got run over and Daddy is about to dispose of the body.]

✿ If you eat your carrots you can see in the dark. [I'm enjoying the fibbing bit now, shameless woman that I am.]

✿ It might sting a bit. [How else am I going to rip this plaster off your knee?]

✿ I asked the lady and she said they'd run out of ice creams. [You are not having an ice cream.]

❁ That cost a lot of money. [It didn't really, but if you break it I might wring your neck.]

❁ I never did drugs/had a one-night stand/got so drunk I lost my shoes … [I think you will find that mothers have their fingers crossed behind their backs when they say any of the above!]

Some mothers deserve Oscars for their inventiveness, as in this case:

> When I was a child, I went through a phase of flicking the lights in our apartment on and off continuously. This was in the early nineties, during the Gulf War, so Mum convinced me to stop by telling me that doing so would send a signal to Saddam to bomb our house. That did the trick.

Another mum told her kids she had a 'catalogue' and that if they were naughty she could trade them in for better-behaved/quieter/tidier models. Perhaps a little harsh, but a genius idea nonetheless, with the added bonus of giving her children an aversion to catalogue shopping in the future.

If you're going on a journey anywhere, mums lie about how long it will take. A 'five'-hour flight to Canada actually takes eight and a half. A 'two'-hour car trip to somewhere in Cornwall takes five.

Mothers resort to lying about all sorts of things, and then justify their actions on the grounds that it's about something important – like getting their children to eat fruit and vegetables. As in: If you don't eat your fruit and vegetables all the poor children in Africa will starve, or your hair will fall out by dinner time, or you'll never grow any taller … Anything we can think of to frighten the living daylights out of them and get them to tuck into their five a day.

Sometimes mothers' fibs come back to bite them. After the

entire house had been searched top to bottom for a 'missing' set of keys, one little boy eventually offered his mother this suggestion: 'I wonder if it might be in the downstairs toilet? I saw a little boy from Africa putting them there.'

Children are much cleverer than mothers think.

THE BIGGEST COLLECTIVE LIE EVER

In the interests of trying to ensure that children are well behaved from one end of the year to the next, mothers and fathers alike have managed to concoct the biggest, most sophisticated *little white lie* ever. (I love that phrase 'little white lie'; either something's a lie or it's not, yet those three words make lying sound innocent – whoever came up with that one must have been a mother.) With Father Christmas we've really gone for it big time and built an entire industry upon it. It has to be the most ambitious lie ever.

The trouble starts when parents begin to embellish the lie. They come up with added details like elves and sleighs and reindeer – even though we all know that the more complicated a lie gets, the more difficult it is to remember. As a result, parents must keep ever so slightly changing their story. And then you find out that friends at school have been given a slightly conflicting story or different answers.

The bloke with bad breath dressed up as Father Christmas in the garden centre was a worry to me even as a child – I never liked the idea of someone like him coming into my bedroom when no one else was around. It's a shame that Santa is Father not Mother Christmas, given that it's usually mums who do most of the shopping. Clever mothers make the whole story work for them, with Father Christmas's spies unmasked as anything and everything from the birds on the bird table to the lollipop lady who watches to check you are crossing the road nicely every day. My grandmother would warn me that a little robin would come to the window to see if I was behaving and report back to Father Christmas. Then she said it would be a blackbird ... and then a sparrow. In no time at all, great big flaws start to open up in the great big lie.

Children suspend their disbelief. Or I did. For an embarrassingly long time, which is something that happens to only children like me. One year I positively definitely heard the reindeer. No, I *really* did – that's how much I believed my parents. My only puzzlement was why Father Christmas gave me so many presents when my own parents only gave me two or three in the afternoon – after all, they were my parents and Father Christmas hadn't even met me.

Logic should tell kids that anyone who can get in and out of so many houses without being seen is more likely to take stuff than give it, but kids play along all the same.

The Santa fib is a crucial training ground for mothers:

Q: Santa has been delivering for hundreds of years – how can he be that old?
A: It's a family business.

Q: There's no way Santa could deliver gifts to every little boy and girl in twenty-four hours.
A: Santa owns the post office. They do most of the deliveries for him, and he personally delivers to the kids who have been extra-good.

See how good mothers are at justifying fibbing to their kids! They just develop this ability to make stuff up, off the cuff. They have an answer, it seems, for everything.

Tooth fairy

As if Father Christmas wasn't enough, parents really push their luck and go for the tooth fairy lie – the logic of which escapes me. Unless it is to encourage children to let you pull their loose teeth out when they are wiggling around. Children divide into two camps: the ones that love fiddling with their loose teeth and pull them out as soon as they're loose, and those that can't bear to touch them, in which case their baby teeth dangle precariously for weeks. Usually parents are desperate to pull them out. Like lancing a boil or popping a blackhead, it's all you can do not to strap them down to pull it out. It's one of the perks of motherhood, being able to pick out head lice, cut a fringe, or toenails or lance the odd boil. Our eldest's front tooth was literally dangling for weeks; she was unable to eat or speak properly. Finally her dad persuaded her to let him pull it out, and he wrapped it in his hankie and gave it a very decisive yank. Only to discover that he was holding two teeth rather than one. I can still picture the shock on her face. And his.

Children are usually very underwhelmed with the idea of the tooth fairy – a fifty-pence piece is hardly worth getting excited about. But it does teach children an important lesson in life: how to play one adult off against another. Only parents who have very little to do make time to compare notes as to how much the tooth fairy leaves behind, thus amounts vary dramatically and are open to abuse. Most of us are as flotsam and jetsam on the tide of the market forces, so if the Rowbottoms pay £10 a tooth I guess we'll have to do the same.

Gooseberry bushes

Sometimes it's not that mothers intend to mislead but more that they are unprepared when the time comes. Because Big Questions have a tendency to come when you least expect them. We were hurrying through a multi-storey car park when my eldest daughter asked me how babies were made; I found myself telling her that 'Daddy has a special stick' – and I thought I was sexually liberated!

Most mums don't want to have this conversation at all. I know there are some who claim to sit down and discuss the ins and outs of all things carnal with their kids as if they're chatting about the weather, but such mums are, without a doubt, ODD. Talking about these things with your mother is seriously creepy. You don't want to imagine she knows anything about it at all.

It is a mother's duty to make the issue as confusing and awkward as possible and, of course, try to put you off ever doing it yourself. Methods range from 'Mum and Dad only did it once, so we could have you' to the old classic 'Playing with your privates will make you go blind' or 'The stork brought you.' One mum cannily told her daughter that having sex made your thighs big. Clever – until they spotted a rather pear-shaped lady in the supermarket and the twelve-year-old daughter exclaimed, 'Look, Mummy, she must be a right slapper.'

There's no right way of doing it. Invariably this results in much cringing and searching for ever more ridiculous names for parts of the body: lady garden/winky/love wand/magic stick/noo noo and front-bottom. Because if Mum ever uses a real, clinical word she will of course start sniggering like a schoolgirl! This is all OK when a girl is five or six, but quite embarrassing for the poor soul who has to be told by her first boyfriend that what's in her knickers isn't called a 'whatsit'.

Of course you could always leave it to the school. After all, they have 'the video' (filmed circa 1967) which is wheeled out into a hushed library to explain matters sexual. (It is of course a well-known fact that in the eighties and nineties primary schools had only three videos: 'Words and Pictures', the 'Train Track Safety' video and the 'Sexual Education' video.) If a child's first image of sex is their sixty-year-old form tutor putting a condom on to a banana, it may well put them off for life. Which might be the idea.

After viewing a film about masturbation in my primary school, one nine-year-old boy put his hand up and asked our teacher, a very brash Scottish lady, 'What does the nice feeling feel like?' That moment, and the look of fear on the teacher's face, has never left me!

The trouble is that mothers and other adults leave huge gaps in their explanations about sex, like the finer details of the docking procedure, or in my case where this hanky-panky took place, which seemed a perfectly reasonable question. Do people do it at work? I wondered. At the garden centre? Because I hadn't grasped that it was such a regular occurrence, I assumed they put it in their diaries when they decided to make babies. It didn't occur to me for a minute it happened in beds. It was only when on holiday, sneaking a look at dirty postcards and finding cartoons of couples in bed that I put two and two together.

Mothers rarely tell the truth to their children. It's not in their nature, and besides they want their children to think, as they do, that they are the best person ever to walk this earth, that if they try hard they can become J.K. Rowling or Bill Gates. They're better than all the other kids and – just remember this – much prettier, cleverer, smarter, from a better home, altogether a step up from everyone else …

Of course, the end result of Mum putting you on a pedestal is that she doesn't want you to let her down.

Mothers need to be good at fibbing – OK, lying – because there is a dark, evil side to motherhood, one that is often born of necessity. Their number one role in life is to protect and nurture their offspring, and nothing must stand in their way. Least of all other people's children.

If we're honest, mothers only really like their own children. Other people's children are only tolerated to keep your own offspring company. As soon as yours have all moved out, children – with the exception of your grandchildren – are pretty irritating. Empty-nest mothers are like ex-smokers, you see. Suddenly you go to a restaurant and bemoan the fact that children are allowed in after 7 p.m., yet wind back ten years and you'd have been aghast at how intolerant your fellow diners were.

How good are mums at pretending they like other children? OK, you're right, not very. When someone else's child sicks up on the back seat of your car, or spills their Ribena on your lovely new white carpet you pretend not to mind. Often not all that well. Worse, other people's children might be sitting their Maths GCSE a year earlier, or get into Cambridge, or be picked for the star role in the play – and yours isn't. What's not to hate? It's all you can do not to wring their necks.

We mothers are ruthless. If we need to be vile to people, we will be. We are quite capable of finger-wagging, bullying and blackmail if we think it will put a stop to our little darling being bullied, or even just left out. We can't help it, it's the way we're wired.

Apart from being good liars and manipulators, mums are incapable of trusting anyone who is in charge of their children at any stage. As far as Mum is concerned, she is the only one that is truly able to look after them well. Babysitters are never trusted, nannies, teachers, bossy friends are all watched, monitored and tested. If CCTV were more widely available, mothers would review the footage with eagle eyes. Then again, most mothers can tell if the nanny has had her friends round for coffee instead of putting a wash on and getting ahead with the ironing while their toddler had an afternoon rest. They just know stuff.

LOUSY FIBBERS

 others are not always good liars, as revealed by these genuine excuses for children's absences from school collected by the Wells Branch School District:

Dear school please accuse John from being absent on January 28, 29, 30, 31, 32, and also 33.

I had to keep Billie home because she had to go Christmas shopping because I didn't know what size she wore.

Please excuse Johnny for being. It was his father's fault.

Mary could not come to school because she was bothered by very close veins.

Maryann was absent December 11–16 because she had a fever, sore throat, headache, and upset stomach. Her sister was also sick, fever and sore throat, her brother had a low grade fever and ached all over. I wasn't the best either, sore throat and fever. There must be the flu going around, her father even got hot last night.

CHILDREN TELL
IT LIKE IT IS

nlike mothers, children are extraordinarily uneconomical with the truth – sometimes painfully so:

What did God make Mummy out of? 'Men's bones and a lot of string.' Briony, four.

What was your mum like as a little girl? 'My mum was never young. Except with the dinosaurs. I think she bossed the T Rex around.' Dawn, five.

What would it take to make your mum perfect? 'On the inside she's already perfect. On the outside, maybe some kind of plastic surgery.' Lois, four.

One five-year-old came downstairs at a family party wearing her mum's Spanx and proclaiming – 'Mummy wears these so she doesn't look as fat as Gran.'

What kind of little girl was your mum?

❀ My mum has always been my mum and none of that other stuff.

❀ I don't know because I wasn't there, but my guess would be pretty bossy.

❀ They say she used to be nice.

Why did your mum marry your dad?

❀ She got too old to do anything else with him.

❀ My grandma says that Mum didn't have her thinking cap on.

❀ 'Because Daddy makes the best pasta. And Mummy eats a lot.'
Tululah, four.

If you could change one thing about your mum, what would it be?

❀ She has this weird thing about me keeping my room clean. I'd get rid of that.

❀ I'd make my mum smarter. Then she would know it was my sister who did it and not me.

❀ I would like for her to get rid of those invisible eyes on the back of her head.

I need my mum when I am Iu or Sick.

My mum always thinks She knows best Sometimes She Ses I know best and Sometimes She does know best.

my mum gets cross with me for doing little things that don't matter.

THINGS THAT MAKE MUMS CRY

others cry at all sorts of stuff. Obviously they cry when anything serious goes wrong for their children, you'd expect that. But motherhood takes it one step further, triggering a cry-at-anything hormone. The tough career woman who wore killer heels to work and could cheerfully reduce a rival to tears in the boardroom becomes pregnant and all of a sudden she's crying at the sight of a lost kitten poster or an advert for loo roll featuring a puppy. Mothers-to-be cry at the weirdest things: on discovering that George Michael was gay, my friend's pregnant mum started crying because 'now he won't have to die alone'.

Mothers weep big time at *Casualty* or *Holby City* or any TV programme about hospitals. They daren't even look at any stories involving children, because they suspend their disbelief to a troubling extent and anything involving sick children is liable to render them inconsolable, clutching wet clumps of tissue, their eyes swollen and red, unable to get a grip on themselves for hours on end. God knows what they'd be like in a real crisis.

Basically mothers are like incendiary devices. One minute they're calm reading *Bella* or in the bath with a nice mug of peppermint tea, and the next they are basket cases, sobbing uncontrollably because they've been watching the Children of Courage awards on TV. The older they get, the more they cry. Anything can set them off: you've let three days go by without texting them back, or they've unearthed a little drawing you did for them when you were at nursery school and put dozens of kisses at the end, or maybe they just caught sight of themselves in the mirror, naked. Mothers are undoubtedly lots of wonderful things, but emotionally well balanced isn't one of them. Not in my experience. Everyday things that most of us would take in our stride – like having a few people round for supper, or putting up an old friend for a couple of nights – is enough to send a mother into La-la Land. Into screaming or sobbing till she's almost sick mode. Mothers have so much to do at any one time that one more little thing can send them over the edge, leaving Dad and the kids to weather the storm.

Sometimes the sobbing happens in public. She promised she wouldn't. Cry, that is. But when the coach pulls out of the school car park, or when it comes back after the school trip, she sobs so much her mascara streams down her face and her face bloats like a puffer fish.

It's not even just the bad stuff she cries about. She greets you at the airport in Arrivals after you've been trekking in India for two months and is a blubbing mess. You give a brilliant performance in the school play (or even a mind-numbingly terrible performance in the school play) and she can be seen sobbing in the front row. I cried through the film *Love Actually* from beginning to end. When I say from beginning to end, I literally started crying at the opening titles and I was still crying at the end credits. It just seemed to reach the very essence of my love for my kids and for family life. I had just been away on a business trip for two weeks, I was jet-lagged and I did miss my family very much, but I probably just needed a good night's sleep.

It's not just mothers' tendency to cry at the big moments, it's all the other times that make her so loveable. My Mum cries at Jennifer Aniston films – every single one. Between sobs she once said to me, 'I don't know why that woman can't keep a boyfriend, she's got brilliant hair,' and that started her off crying again.

Mums will cry at everything. Fact. Here's some things that make them cry:

✿ Not being able to work the TV/car/microwave/radio/shower/ tin opener
✿ Leaving milk off the shopping list
✿ Seeing babies of any kind – even the ugly ones
✿ Not being able to decide what to eat
✿ *The X Factor*
✿ Clouds
✿ The cat not wanting a cuddle
✿ Finding a new stretch mark
✿ The state Lindsay Lohan's got herself in
✿ Seeing a kid drop his ice cream
✿ Getting a hair band caught in your hair
✿ Watching people at Arrivals in Terminal 3
✿ The national anthem
✿ Onions
✿ Brass bands
✿ Bisto ads
✿ Anything in their keepsake drawer
✿ Nativity plays
✿ Nursery rhymes
✿ Small children singing

Weddings are the BIG one on the crying front. One mum I know cried from the moment she woke up to the moment she went to bed on her daughter's wedding day; everything set her off: the hairdresser arriving, putting on the dress – Oh My God, putting on the dress – but that was nothing compared to when the music started in the church. I have no idea why mother of the bride outfits don't come with veils to hide the blotchy swollen faces that they end up with. And just wait till they get the video of the wedding home. Hours and hours at home weeping and wailing all over again.

They make one another worse too. Watching other mums cry seems to set them off big time, so two mums watching a wedding video = howling and crying so much their shoulders go up and down. Which is why a royal wedding is the World Cup of crying for women – I found myself crying when Kate took her father's hand to walk down the aisle. And when 'Jerusalem' came on I was blubbing like I was in infants school. I have no idea why, because I don't even like the monarchy; in fact, I think they are a waste of food.

Being a mother involves a great deal of crying, even though most of the time we have no idea why we are crying at all.

MUMS AND BIRTHDAYS

others, as usual, set their expectation-bar far too high and want their children's birthdays to be perfect, which can only mean one thing: they will be impossible to live with for weeks – it's the lead-up to Christmas all over again.

The first problem is who to invite to the party. When the children are small there are so many daily squabbles and falling outs that they either invite the whole class or three best friends. Their best friends change on a daily basis, with considerable emotional fallout, and so you have no choice but to invite the whole class. Do the maths and you can see the problem: you invite the entire class, all twenty-eight of them, plus one or two cousins and big sister's (current) best friend. Dozens of children invade your house, dropped off by parents who, having just been given the afternoon off, can't get away fast enough – with the exception of a few clingy mothers who offer to 'help', which is code for: I'm going to police this party and ensure that my little Chloe wins at least one of the games and if there is a health and safety issue I'll be there to raise it. Even the cleverest, most level-headed of mothers have trouble dealing with this scenario. Within minutes children are running up and down the stairs, crying, feeling left out, and being mean to your birthday girl or boy.

The other problem is that children realise they can get away with almost ANYTHING on their birthdays. All the usual rules go out of the window. They're the birthday boy/girl, they even have the badge to prove it; they are officially allowed to be badly behaved. They can climb on/write on/eat/drink anything they choose and as Mum, you will look like the antichrist if you reduce them to tears on their special day.

One friend's mum was told off by her eldest child under precisely these circumstances. On friend's third birthday, Mum came downstairs to discover that she had taken off her nappy and smeared its contents over the whole living room. Her five-year-old sister nonchalantly turned to her poor mother and said, 'It's Claire's birthday ... she can play in her own poo if she wants.' I think that sums the whole day up nicely.

As usual, stop-at-home mums and working mums approach birthdays in totally different ways. Working mothers hire jugglers, take the week off work, and generally wear themselves out to prove that work doesn't prevent them being a model mum. As a result they hit the gin by the time the cake is cut and it's tears before bedtime – for Mum that is, not the birthday girl. Non-working mothers are much cleverer. They pace themselves, and don't need to prove anything. They probably manage to supervise some Kumon Maths homework the day before, and don't do anything fancy.

As a new mother you make big birthday party mistakes. My own spectacular one was misspelling Rebecca's name on her first birthday cake. All I can say is that I had a lot to do. But the mistakes don't end there. You learn with experience: birthday parties are easily categorised by how many children you have and how many children's parties you have thrown.

Invitations
❖ **First Child:** Drawn by hand, coloured and printed by Mum at work, and put in the memory drawer when the party is over.
❖ **Second Child:** From a pad of standard Clinton's birthday invites.

✿ **Third Child:** Put the word around.

Timings

✿ **First Child:** 2–6.30 p.m. As a first-time mum you make the party last far too long. You've done some pre-tea games, you've had tea – in fact, tea took about five minutes because they were only really interested in crisps and chocolate Rice Krispie cakes and you can wolf those down in a second – and you still have two hours to amuse them/keep them alive until parents come to collect them.

✿ **Second Child:** 4–6 prompt. Just enough time to wear them out, feed them, and cut the cake.

✿ **Third Child:** 5–6. Anyone left unpicked up after that helps to clear up the hall.

Location

✿ **First Child:** At home. Grandparents, friends and professionals are drafted in, there have been rehearsals, everything is filmed for posterity.

✿ **Second Child:** Half the house is out of bounds.

✿ **Third Child:** A church hall. Mum brings dry white wine.

Dress

✿ **First Child:** Fancy dress. Mum makes a Princess Leia costume, Dad hires a giant Dalmatian outfit. People go over the top. Twins arrive as two palm trees connected by a hammock. You get the picture.

✿ **Second Child:** You buy them a nice new party dress.

✿ **Third Child:** Sister's party dress and like it.

Food

✿ **First Child:** Ribena in paper cups for tea, which are knocked over by the dozen and spill on the beige carpet. Mum wears herself out trimming the sandwiches into star shapes, and providing some healthy crudités and dips. Then twenty-eight children descend and eat only two things: the crisps and the sausages.

✿ **Second child:** Orange squash, sausage rolls, ham sandwiches and chocolate sponge rolls.

✿ **Third child:** Crisps with cake for afters. Tap water.

Cake

✿ **First child:** Mum follows a recipe, hires a cake tin, and has a dry run. She might build a log cabin out of chocolate fingers and marshmallows, or fashion a cake in the shape of a pony.

✿ **Second child:** Bought from the local bakers and decorated with name and age and some candles.

✿ **Third child:** Tesco's chocolate cake. One candle fits all.

Party bags

✿ **First child:** You've bagged and named them all, they sit in a pretty basket with a bow on, you've spent more on little knick-knacks that will be thrown away or eaten before they get home than you would repeat to anyone. You give everyone a piece of cake in a themed serviette to take home and pop it in their party bags, but you don't forbid them to eat it until they have left the building and so thirty-two pieces of chocolate cake are eaten while running amok, waiting for their parents to arrive.

✿ **Second child:** A piece of cake in a serviette that they are forbidden to eat until they leave.

✿ **Third child:** You don't believe in party bags and claim they are bad for children's morality.

Games

✿ **First child:** There is an elaborate schedule, with each game having a special wrapped prize, climaxing in the judging of the fancy dress. Musical chairs, musical statues, pass-the-parcel with presents in each layer, with only the thirty minutes of professional 'entertainment' to allow Mum and Dad to take some photos. Some parents give in and allow murder in the dark.

- ❀ **Second Child:** Musical statues with Dad on the stop button knowing who the troublemakers are (not bumps: a trip to A&E ensued last time), pass-the-parcel with newspaper wrappers and a really crap present inside.
- ❀ **Third Child:** 'There's the hall, get on with it.'

Clever ideas (not)

- ❀ **First Child:** 'It's November, it's nearly Bonfire Night … I know, let's do a firework display in the garden.' It's not until you try to get thirty-two kids outside with the right pairs of wellies, hats, gloves and their coats buttoned up and get them to stand behind the line you drew on the lawn that you realise what a stupid idea this was. You'll be lucky not to get sued by litigious parents.
- ❀ **Second Child:** A trip to the bowling alley and then back home for tea. Try walking thirty kids across town, or ferrying them in cars.
- ❀ **Third Child:** 'Go out and play.'

Mum after the party is over

- ❀ **First Child:** A day off work to recover, a nasty hangover, a fridge full of ham sandwiches and a pile of really horrible presents that birthday girl was given.
- ❀ **Second Child:** She did nothing else all weekend.
- ❀ **Third Child:** She skipped Zumba.

other people's children

The other shock about hosting birthday parties is being in charge of other people's children, when you don't much like other people's children. They come in distinct varieties:

❀ The little git who you have to keep your eye on the whole time.

❀ Mummy's Little Princess – whose mum's last words on the doorstep are, 'Have fun, remember the dress is DRY CLEAN ONLY.' She will probably burst into tears once or twice.

❀ The smarty-pants child, who points out how the magician is doing all of his tricks.

❀ The one with the allergy to nuts will inevitably keep straying near the Snickers

and someone will always be crying.

Presents

Mothers can be the meanest people on earth especially when it comes to giving people (other than their own children) gifts. Their generosity is very measured. The kids come home from a birthday party and the first thing mothers ask is what did birthday girl get from the other kids? Not because she's interested, but because she's measuring whether she's overdone or underdone the present and will adjust with mathematic accuracy next time. Same with your own birthday. She's making mental notes of exactly who is giving you recycled gifts or crap that came from the charity shop. She's doing this, by the way, because *she can tell.*

Mothers are obsessed with re-gifting. They save things in a special drawer for this purpose; these are the items she's tried to take back for a refund and failed, that's how bad they are. The more expensive the wrapping she puts on it, the worse it is – and the more ashamed she is of it.

If you have more than one child you might indulge in the un-birthday present tradition. Every birthday for child A must be offset by an 'un-birthday' present for child B, lest the second be offended by the fact the first one had been born. But the present can't be too extravagant or the birthday girl will think you're showing favouritism. Neither can it be too stingy, or it will look as though you don't love them as much. That's before you've even got to the one whose birthday it is. And the un-birthday sibling has to get to invite a friend to the party too – and it's always one that their sister hates. So a little 'rigging' of the music on pass-the-parcel ensures this 'party crasher' never wins a prize or all hell will break loose.

Sensible mums have a strict budget for present-buying, which is equal for each daughter, each year. Even down to the last penny, presents must be equal. Thus each year the unwrapping is supplemented by a running commentary:

'Now I was going to get you the blue one, but your sister only had a Trike, so you'll have to make do.'

'Now this present is just a joke one, cos we had 23p left over and didn't know what to do with it.'

Sleepovers

Only the most self-destructive mother will say yes to a sleepover. 'Sleepover' is in fact a cunning form of childhood slang. Sleep is not involved. While the dictionary definition might be 'an instance of spending the night as a guest at another person's home', the teenage definition is 'a chance to watch all the *Saw* films, nick cider out of the fridge, vomit in the pot plants and call boys you fancy at three in the morning'. Children who are still awake at 3am are up to no good and most of it is going to involve some rubber gloves and a bucket the next day. It was at a sleepover that I had my first taste of alcohol. We carefully snuck the bottles out of the cabinet with excitement only comparable to Christmas Day or a holiday in Disney World, but then discovered what whisky actually tasted like ... and hurriedly topped it up from the Coke bottle and put it back where we found it.

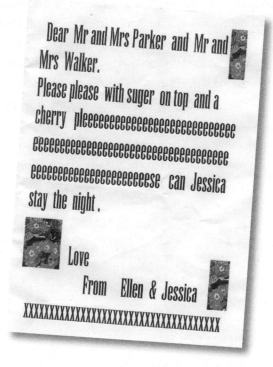

Dear Mr and Mrs Parker and Mr and Mrs Walker.
Please please with suger on top and a cherry pleeeeeeeeeeeeeeeeeeeeeeeeeeeeeeeeeeeeeeeeeeeeeeeeeeeeeeeeeeeeeeeeeeeeeeeeeeeeese can Jessica stay the night.

Love
From Ellen & Jessica
XXXXXXXXXXXXXXXXXXXXXXXXXXXXXXXXXXXXXXXXXX

Mums and their own birthdays

All mums adhere to the mantra that their children's birthdays must be on a ceremonial par with royal weddings, but their own are always approached with the phrase, 'Oh, don't mind me, I don't

want any fuss.' When it comes to Mum's big day, she never wants a
'fuss'. Even if she's turning fifty. Even if it's her last birthday before the
kids move abroad for work. Mums say really unhelpful things like,
'Oh, love, just seeing you is present enough.' When you ask them
what they want, they ask for mad things like (actual examples):

* An outside light for the front garden.
* A flowery dustpan and brush.
* Super Strength Bathroom Cleaner.
* A towel.
* A spatula.

I genuinely think that some mums would be happier to get a dirty
kitchen to clean for their birthday than a nice piece of jewellery.

Dear Mum,

Happy Birthday!!!
I tried to find a
Stupid picture of you
to stick on this card
but there is a surprising
lack of them.... even
though you do do stupid
things when EVERYONES
looking!! lots of love
Ellen
xxx

P.S. I know I nicked this card
from your draw.... :)

DOS AND DON'TS WITH MUM

DO

✔ Go home for Christmas. [Not to do so is punishable by death.]

✔ Be safe. [Just … you know, in general.]

✔ Put washing in the basket.

✔ Tell her she's the best mum in the world. Better still, tell her all your mates think she's a great mum. [Unless she regularly allows raves or sleepovers that involve the entire house they won't ever say that, but watch her turn to putty in your hands.]

✔ Agree with her. [It's for your own good.]

✔ Play dumb about sex. [If you don't understand it, you can't be doing it.]

✔ Bribe her with cups of tea. [Tea is mothers' answer to cocaine.]

✔ Wipe your feet when you come in the front door. Even better, ask your mates to do that while she is listening.

✔ Take one of the little piles she has left at the bottom of the stairs to take up upstairs. [NB make sure she sees.]

✔ Tell her you're sorry. [There will always be something you should be sorry for.]

✔ Go to her when you unexpectedly need greeting cards – bereavement/belated birthday/get well soon … [She has them all and will think she's brought you up well.]

✔ Tell her she looks younger than Rosie's mum. [You know Rosie's mum is young because she still has stabilisers on her bike.]

✔ Confide in her. [Nothing very revealing, obviously, but mothers really like this.]

DON'T

✘ Think that you'll get away with it … whatever IT is.

✘ Look at a photo of her in her twenties and say, 'I didn't recognise you.'

✘ Compare her to anyone on *Loose Women*.

✘ Correct her on the names of singers. [She'll still go on calling them Justin Beaver/Mrs Gaga/Take This.]

✘ Say 'Nan does that better' or point out how much she looks like Nan.

✘ Write on the walls, pick at the wallpaper or do anything that might involve redecorating.

✘ Tickle her. [Mothers can't deal with being tickled.]

✘ Frighten her by saying you want to take up anything dangerous.

✘ Nick her alcohol if you haven't planned an appropriate substance to top it up with.

✘ Expect her to forget. [As the saying goes: She can forgive …]

✘ Make her feel guilty. [She does that enough to herself.]

✘ Forget to record *Strictly*.

GOD SHE'S EMBARRASSING

Mothers are embarrassing. It's part of their job description. Mothers who are not embarrassing are not real mothers at all. Whether they're eating from their tragic Tupperware under the pub table, demanding to see the manager in Sainsbury's, or walking along the landing in their grey baggy underwear, it's bad.

But it's really bad when she dances.

My own daughters do a terrifyingly accurate impression of me dancing, mouthing to the words of 'West End Girls' or 'Sisters Are Doin' It for Themselves'. It doesn't make a difference if she's naked or not. Not, preferably. My youngest's verdict on me on the dance floor is: 'Her dancing. Indescribable. I always wonder if she danced like that when she was my age or if it's something she developed through age. Either way, I often pretend we're not related at parties.'

My children's friends also do cunningly accurate impressions of their own mothers dancing. Presumably they have perfected these impressions in order to avoid their own dancing looking anything like it. I (evidently) have an embarrassing tendency to keep my mouth slightly open while clicking my fingers in a way that has hints of Dame Edna, or a drag artist. Not that I care a jot. Sometimes, when everyone is in, and it's a Friday night, and the girls are cuddled up watching *Friends* – or, let's face it, more likely *Sex in the City* – the old man's not annoying me too much, and one

Is she dancing now? I can't look.

of my favourite tracks comes on, say a Tina Turner, I'll just turn it up and dance in the kitchen. Motherhood just takes you like that sometimes. To have all the family under my roof, nice and safe and near and snuggled in. But I do realise that this is a scary sight. I don't dance like my own mother, hers is more a matter of bringing one foot over to the other and back again in a side-to-side way, mine is much more energetic and flamboyant and, well ... more embarrassing.

Embarrassing mum dancing is in the genes, latently waiting there to embarrass future generations. I know that because the other day my daughter texted me to say that she was dancing to the Pointer Sisters and thinks she was doing a mum dance.

other embarrassing stuff mothers do

✿ Putting their hands up and asking questions at parents evenings.
✿ Getting words wrong. Being incapable of using the word

'random' properly.

- 🌸 Trying to be one of the gang or down with the kids.
- 🌸 Swooning over James Morrison.
- 🌸 Kissing you in public.
- 🌸 Crying in public.
- 🌸 Smelling the top of your head.
- 🌸 Telling you they love you in public.
- 🌸 Embarrassing goodbyes: running alongside blowing kisses at railway stations.
- 🌸 Jumping around, unable to contain her excitement, when the school-trip coach returns to school.
- 🌸 Sending your mac into school in case it rains.
- 🌸 Meeting your latest boy/girlfriend and saying, 'At last, a normal one!'
- 🌸 Crying at weddings. Anyone's.
- 🌸 Mum jeans. Nuff said.

Oh, and there's her temper. Make that rage. She's the shopper from hell. One tiny little thing goes wrong and she goes into a top-of-the-range rant. She doesn't even have the courtesy to build up to it so that you have time to scarper or run for cover. Mothers are quite capable of a hand-on-hip slanging match at the customer services till at Tesco. Oh yes. Quite capable. She will also dump anything she's changed her mind about buying anywhere – bacon by the washing powder, taramasalata by the tinned fruit … Mothers are fearless and utterly without shame.

She Facebook stalks your friends. And when she meets them, she will mention things she could only know through Facebook, and will call them by whatever nickname you use when describing them to her.

She STILL likes to give you a kiss on the cheek just after she's put her lipstick on. It was embarrassing when you were eight, it's worse now.

She also stage whispers instead of actual whispering if she is commenting on someone who looks awful in whatever they are wearing. CRINGE.

No matter how old you are, she will ask if you've been to the loo before you go anywhere or do anything. And if you haven't she'll say, 'Can you just try?' Mothers remain in charge of everyone's toilet habits. Mums who return to work are prone to ask people in the office if they have washed their hands properly.

Dear Mum, the most Lovely and Special mum in the universe,

you're my perfect mummy, and I love you very much, even though you're 47 and your Farts are revolting, Smelly, disgusting, Fowl, gross, pongy and Loud!!

Happy 47th Birthday!!!

Love
Ellen
x++

P.S. your poo's are revolting too!!

THAT GLASS OF WINE HAS GONE STRAIGHT TO MY HEAD

Mothers can't take their drink. That's an official scientific fact. Once we've given birth, gone through hormonal hell, then had years of not being able to sleep through the night, we find ourselves in dire need of dry white wine. Trouble is, we can no longer take our booze. Little by little our tolerance for alcohol dwindles away until eventually we have a glass of sweet sherry before Sunday lunch or Christmas dinner and we go bright red and forget the Yorkshire puds. Whatever happens, you can be sure of one thing: mothers do embarrassing stuff when they're a bit tipsy.

Tipsy Mothers get very confessional. They start to relish the look of horror on your face at stories of boyfriends they had before your dad and the male friends of yours who have been secretly giving them a wink. Only one thing is harder to cope with than a Tipsy Mother and that is a group of them. A gaggle of Tipsy Mothers. A flock of Tipsy Mothers. A pride of them, all kicking their heels in the air, revelling in your embarrassment and reminiscing about who they lost their virginity to.

Drunken mums give great, if blunt advice. My best friend's mum told us at eighteen: 'Don't have kids, girls, it ruins your social life and your figure.' And then she flounced away, totally forgetting her own daughter was in the room.

They invariably do things they regret, like sending emails to all the people who have been annoying them that day/week/life. They get a bit randy, which in a mum is never a good look. I have heard tales of woe from daughters whose names appear next to their father's in their mum's phone and so have mistakenly been sex-texted. And as everyone knows, a fruity mother should only ever mean one who is preparing jam.

A truly tiddled mum is something you'll probably only see once or twice a year, but it is a sight to behold. Once she thinks, 'Oh, sod it, the kids are old enough now!' there's no stopping her.

The yearly drunk mother's appearance tends to deteriorate through the night. It's at these times she tends to ask those questions she might have otherwise felt unable to. In front of a packed pub, one otherwise conservative mum asked her daughter: 'I'd just been wondering, love, if you might be a lesbian?'

Of course you can use mum's tiddliness to your own advantage. It's the perfect time to ask for money. Or to use the car. Or to remind her that she *did* say you could go to Glastonbury and take half your sister's wardrobe with you. Technically, it's exploitation, but really it's more a case of 'picking your moment'.

Then there is the drunken rant. Mums can suddenly feel very politically/socially motivated after three glasses of wine. But whereas some drunks might tackle war, poverty or injustice, drunken mums like to concentrate on how Mrs Johnson at number 18 really is a nosy cow, or how the council don't collect the bins enough, or worst of all how no one appreciates what she does.

Some typical mum rants are as follows:
❀ People taking her parking space
❀ Noisy eaters

- There being no milk left at Tesco's
- Dog muck on the street (How did it get there? How can we stop it?)
- Neighbours who do DIY at the weekend
- When they move the Soaps because of the football
- The cat from next door who wees in our garden

Even world events can be brought down to a mum ranting level. Everyone knows that once you're a mother your priority is your own home and family. So much so that when Hurricane Katrina hit, the response of a friend's mum was: 'God, how awful. That reminds me, they still haven't fixed our leaky roof.'

Scary mums

Scary mums are like drunken or dancing mums but worse, as they are embarrassing round the clock. Scary mums wear their hair in plaits, or favour strange frilly bouffant skirts in purple, and have dozens of wrist bands. Sometimes they skip. Very scary indeed.

other people's mothers

Are entirely different. When they do embarrassing stuff, it's just funny.

YOUR CHILDREN EMBARRASSING YOU

Be prepared to be humiliated, embarrassed and maybe even a bit taken aback by the things you had no idea children could say. The things they come out with will shock even the most unshockable mothers. Don't tell them anything that you don't want repeated. You might think they will forget, but they won't. They have encyclopaedic memories when it comes to embarrassing stuff. They have no shame. Things you once said in passing will become weapons to be used against you to get you to do things you had no intention of doing. Bribes, for instance. Do not think that you can dangle any sort of bribe without delivering on the promise, not unless you want to be subjected to some serious public humiliation by your child.

Never ever tell them you are hoping that Granny will leave you that big diamond ring she wears, or that you think the bloke next door might be a ladyboy. Your kids will tell both Granny and the bloke next door.

Children make some wonderfully embarrassing mistakes. Like this sticker story by a little boy – it was just one letter that he missed out, but it made all the difference:

HORES

I like hores. Hores have other hores frinds.
Hores like carrots. You wouldn't think they
could but they can put thir legs strait up.
Hores make you feel good My Dad wants
a hores but my mum says no. When I am
16 or 20 I will buy my own hores.

MUMS ON HOLIDAY

Mothers want – no, make that *need* – family holidays to be perfect and for everyone to get on like a house on fire for a full fortnight.

They need the whole family to be blissfully happy because they know how precious family holidays are. All too soon their children will turn into teenagers who would rather be anywhere on earth other than with their parents on holiday. I once went on a canoeing holiday in France and saw a canoe being paddled in the blistering heat by two fifty-year-old parents with their teenage daughter lolling on the front reading *Hello!* magazine – the unspoken truth being that parents want their children to be on holiday with them more than children want to be on holiday with their parents.

The result of all this, no matter what age your children are, is that mothers wear themselves out ragged on holiday trying to make sure everyone is happy. And they do this just when they are so worn out from working the whole year leading up to it that they can barely speak a civil word to anyone.

Despite mothers needing holidays to be perfect, they never are. You can never find the right place to camp, there is always a fornicating couple within earshot or a radio blaring, or topless girls, or a dog licking its genitals or a bin crawling with wasps. Then there are rip tides to worry about, common people with nasty dogs off leads, and broken glass to cut your foot open on. As a result mothers wear themselves out (even more than normal) moving rooms, complaining to reception or the rep, and pretending they haven't heard the fornicating couple next door. If it rains, the board games come out, and there is only so much Ludo or Junior Scrabble a mother can take before boiling over like a pressure cooker.

All too often, mums work just as hard on holiday as they do the rest of the year. Unless you are staying in five-star accommodation, mothers do all the same chores but with a really small kitchen and not enough pots and pans; factor in some bad weather, or being near a nightclub, and mothers can be seriously difficult to holiday with.

On the whole, mothers are very conservative about their holiday requirements – they prefer to stay put than to tour, since touring means you can never properly unpack. And mothers like to unpack. They like to get everything out of their case into as many drawers and shelves as possible, and then they feel they've nested. They are at home.

Mothers do not like holidays that involve any of the following words: rafting, trekking, orienteering, jumping, malaria, or extreme … Nor do they much like their children going on holidays involving these words. But their children have different ideas. Sometimes people persuade mums to go on holidays where an element of danger is involved – camels, cable cars, skiing, pony trekking – they do this just so that they can watch mums in what they consider to be dangerous situations. It's a seriously entertaining spectator sport. Watch a mum ride an elephant or camel and you will not be disappointed. My mother was terrified of cable cars, so if we ever went on one, she'd talk to herself. However it was not just talking – she'd say physics equations to herself. Needless to say, my father ensured that every holiday we went on involved cable cars becasue the floor show was so entertaining.

Mothers are rubbish at relaxing so it's not going to change a fat lot when they are on holiday. Not unless you can tank a mother up with some tequila (and most people do). No, on holiday her bodyguard duties are on full red alert round the clock. She will have done some research – googling via the Foreign Office website for trouble spots, natural disasters and killer diseases. Trouble is, once she gets to the villa/hotel/dump there are extra worries like tripping hazards, cloudy water in the swimming pool and some dodgy characters on the beach to worry about. Even the mini disco is run by a bloke who she considers too dodgy to trust while she's having her pudding, and least of all the kids club designed to allow her to leave the kids for hours on end while she lolls by the pool is – she decides – run by young girls who shouldn't be trusted with a pair of scissors. Not even the plastic safety ones.

There is one place, however, that mums forget they are bodyguards. On a sunlounger. Once mothers get on holiday all they want to do is lie on a sunlounger, and they want to lie on it for as long as possible. I for one do not belittle women who bagsy sunloungers before breakfast. Being in possession of a sunlounger is seriously important for a mother. Once mum is on her sunlounger she is formally, legally, off duty and entitled to pass over responsibility for the kids to Dad. Mothers have a world-class talent for this. It's a gift. Both she and Dad might be working full time, but the moment they get to the sunloungers Mum flakes out for the annual inertia big time. She deserves the rest more than he does. Obviously. She's worn herself out ragged getting ready to come on holiday and cleared her inbox at work and now all she's capable of doing is lolling on a sunbed. Which suits her just fine. She can't even be bothered to read; mothers just want to lie there watching the waves and listening to some James Morrison, and chilling out. They can't be arsed to build sandcastles and they certainly can't be arsed to go and look at ruins or temples. Any man knows the only way to get a mum off her sunlounger is the offer of lunch or some bargains at a market. Otherwise forget it. Mum will be there till the sun goes down.

Being on holiday with your mother often means sharing a room – or at the very least a bathroom – with her. This means that you get to see your mother in the nude. Obviously she won't give a monkey's about that, but it may just scar you mentally for life. If you're a daughter, you can see for yourself what is going to happen to your body. I remember seeing my mother in a bathing costume for the first time on the beach circa 1966 and it was before bikini waxes. All I can say is that I have never seen so much pubic hair on show in my life.

Extreme Parenting

Mums who insist on caravan holidays are a breed apart. I consider this Extreme Parenting, the kind of holiday you select in order to push yourself to your limits.

As someone who serially holidayed in caravans as a kid there are three golden rules …

1. Never speak to Mum when she is trying to park the caravan.
2. Never complain about the state of the toilet in the caravan.
3. Never try to hit your sister and make it look like it's an accident in the caravan (it's far too small and Mum will always see you).

Caravanning holidays are not for the tired. It takes about five hours to reach caravan destination, two days to park the caravan, three days to put up the awning, one day to move the caravan when you realise your next-door neighbours remind you of Fred and Rose West, two more days to work out how to use the gas hob – and then it's time to pack up and come home again.

Things mothers take away on holiday

Some mums are also astoundingly stingy on holidays – it's one thing to choose half-board but quite another to sacrifice packing a bikini so that you can stow away a week's worth of baked beans and tea bags.

In order to be prepared for every eventuality, mums insist on bringing a variety of items that have hitherto reposed in a cupboard, unused and unwanted. Some of the weirdest things mums have been known to pack on holiday are:

✿ Ice bags
✿ Spare bikini fasteners
✿ Flat-packed pillows
✿ Paint brush (to get sand out from between toes)
✿ Glade plug-in air freshener
✿ Pegs and portable clothes line
✿ Muesli
✿ Fold-up tool kit
✿ Hot-water bottle (to Tenerife)
✿ Slippers

Sadly all the tension and anxiety surrounding family holidays, coupled with the scary amount of uninterrupted time mums and dads spend together, make them hothouses for split-ups.

One woman remembers:

My parents used family holidays as a countdown to divorce. Florida Mark One was the first test, Mallorca '94 was best remembered by the Argument in which Mum Broke the Bedroom Cabinet and they finally decided to divorce outside of Blizzard Beach at Disney World in 1997. The conversation went roughly like this:

LITTLE SISTER (crying): They're going to diiiivvvvooooorrrrcccce!

ME: No they won't. Shut up.

MUM: Actually, we are. Should we do Magic Kingdom next, or Sea World?

MOTHERS AND PETS

Some mothers have 'allergies' to pets. When I say that word I put it in *Friends*-type inverted commas because these clever mothers have worked out that having an allergy is the best way to get out of having pets. An allergy to fur, for instance, gets you out of most varieties. I know of at least one mother who claimed she had an allergy to fish. Which I think is pushing it a bit, but she got away with it.

Working mothers predictably give in to pets more than the stay-at-homes, adding even more to their appalling workloads and potential for grumpy behaviour from morning to night. They feel guilty that they're not full-time mums, so they prolong their children's childhoods by having pets. Although obviously their kids lose interest in them almost immediately.

My children basically treated their pets like dolls – the hamsters were given wedding ceremonies complete with 'Here Comes the Bride' on the recorder, and Pip the family lab was regularly dressed up.

Sawdust animals

If mothers are forced to give in to a pet then caged animals are obviously first choice. Cages are good – in fact, why stop at animals?

There is no mother on earth who once or twice would not have paid good money for a child-friendly cage.

Sadly, the sawdust involved in caged pets is a high price to pay for pets not roaming round the house. As anyone who has tried to hoover up urine-soaked sawdust, or live with trails of it on carpets will know. Naturally, when mothers agree to a small caged pet, they insist that it should live outside just by the back door. But the day you get the pet home, your children point out how cold it is, and how they need to settle in, and you bring the cage indoors for the first night ... And guess what: the animal never sleeps outside – ever.

You choose these pets because really your children wanted a cat or more likely a dog and you couldn't face the prospect, so you all compromise on a rodent. Unfortunately, rodents are either nocturnal, dull, downright vicious or all three and it's not long before Mum is googling the lifespan of the average guinea pig. I was stupid enough to be talked into pet rats. For an otherwise intelligent woman, my soppy mummy side really gets me into some scrapes, and the pet rats were a good example. Rats turned out to be unaffectionate, revolting, but worst of all devilishly intelligent. You don't really want intelligence in a rodent. It's not a plus, because if they're intelligent they find a way of escaping. Our rats were very crafty. They wouldn't instantly leap to the cage door once they saw it being prepared for opening, they'd hang back like they weren't that fussed while you got really brazen about it and fiddled with changing the stinking water or chucking some food in, and then they'd time it so that you turned your back for a second … then quick as a flash they'd make a run for it. They wouldn't even do it the same every time, totally outwitting us. I lost count of the number of floorboards we had to get up to find them.

Gerbils are escapologists and vicious with it, quite capable of cannibalism. Our friends had two in a cage and when one got ill the other one started to eat it. It didn't even wait till it was dead, just gone a bit quiet. They're also good at biting people and not letting go, which if you are bitten on the nose, as my neighbour's boy was, is distressing.

Cats are the next pet campaign up the food chain. Unfortunately, they can't be kept in a cage and soon the house is a minefield of 'little presents' they leave for you as their much-loved owners. Mice, birds, bats, half-eaten rabbits all are met by the children with screams and will result in the kind of mopping up that involves disposable rubber gloves, or occasionally burial in the garden.

Dead pets are yet another time consumer for mums. Even the most neglected, dreariest of pets can require a fully fledged funeral, when Mum would frankly be happy with flushing or humane disposal involving a black bin liner and the boot of the car. Our garden looks like the Somme there are so many burial plots, which can lead to unexpected emotional fallout as a result of a living pet deciding to dig up a dead one.

We were stupid enough to agree to orphan lambs for a while, bottle-feeding them until they grew into dull old sheep that doubled as lawnmowers. One of them became ill which naturally caused huge upset (despite the fact that we regularly ate roast lamb) and yours truly had to deal with the corpse while the kids were at school. The only thing I could find to put it in was one of those big blue IKEA bags and once rigor mortis set in it didn't quite fit, so it had its tail sticking out the end of it. The vet told me to bring it in to the surgery in case it had died of something infectious, so I walked it over Safeway's car park with a tea towel draped over the bit sticking out of the end feeling like a badly equipped serial killer. The vet charged me about £100 for a post mortem, which helped nobody, and we ended up burying it like all the others in the pet cemetery.

Inevitably, as a busy working mother I was bound to give in to a dog sooner or later. There's a bit of me that thinks, Well, if you're going to have a pet you might as well get one that sits on your lap and likes you. But guess who will be picking up the poo? I have never, ever seen a child pick up dog poo. That's because mothers walk dogs, but also because mothers deal with poo full stop. It's part of the job description – anyone who can do nappies can do dog poo. Some mothers I know take the family dog or puppies to the school gates. This trumps everything. You could collect by helicopter on a daily basis and this would be completely outshone by a mother who brings a dog, or a puppy to the school gates. That is true status.

Puppies are about a hundred times more work than children, and anyone who has had children will realise that's a lot of work. A naughty puppy is like a toddler, but with about four times the strength and without any prospect of potty training. Also it's very hard to smack puppies in public. It is frowned upon even more than smacking a small child – they can probably put you in prison for it.

We made the mistake of picking the lively one in the litter. Unfortunately, opting for the one with all the personality is a big mistake. My advice if you are going to get one is to pick the quiet little petrified one in the corner that will do as it's told. I tell you this because otherwise one day you will be walking your puppy or small dog in the park and it won't come back. You can whistle and shout and run for it all you like, but if it doesn't want to come back it sure as hell will not. Even more humiliating than threatening a small toddler in public with the counting backwards and demanding it stops when you get to zero, puppies who do not do what they're told are truly maddening. You can't even bribe them with stopping up late.

There are mothers, a species all of their own, who agree to horses. Well what can I say? You are from a different gene pool to me, and the only explanation I can come up with is that you wanted a horse even more than your children did, or you are so rich you can afford grooms. We borrowed a horse for a weekend in the hope

My dream Pony

Name: Snowflake
Breed: Welsh Mountin
Colour: White
Sex: Female
Where it likes to be stroked: On her nose.
Its favourite food: Pony mix/carrots.
Is it tame?: Yes, very
Colour of eyes: Bright blue
How much would you Love it: Infinitie %.
Does it come to your call?: Yes
Is he/she obiediant?: Yes, very
When you go to the field where he/she is, how does he/she greet you?: She canters up to me and nibbles my hair.

that it would put our girls off having one, having been subjected to a full-on campaign for a pony for a good twelve months. It did the trick: they went off the idea in less than twenty-four hours. Horses are a full-time job. The sheer size and strength of the bloody things is a shock; they churned our little field up into a quagmire within a day, and by the Sunday afternoon the girls were both too done in to put the hay out or whatever it is they eat. No; borrowing or hiring other people's pets is the way forward. If only you could hire dogs by the afternoon. Now that's a sound business idea.

Pets do extend your children's childhood, that much is true. There is nothing like buying a thirteen-year-old girl a puppy for delaying her interest in boys, clubbing and *Cosmo* magazine. But get real, it won't last. If you are thinking of getting a pet and your children are over five think on this: do you want to be walking a greying Labrador or poodle with halitosis and a gammy leg when the kids have gone off to university? You may be writing them newsy emails about Lady, but believe me they will *so* have moved on.

MUMS AND PETS LIST

The ugly truth about mothers who have pets:

❀ The notion of liberating animals into the wild has occurred to every mother – some of us have even said it out loud when the guinea pigs need cleaning out, there's a family holiday to prepare for and everyone has lost interest. Unfortunately, children see through this.

❀ Mothers are incapable of picking up small animals, and often pets themselves. Most would prefer to cuddle their children.

❀ Pets are to children what flowers, a cuddle in front of the fire, or a great big fat compliment is to a mother. Pets are their currency.

❀ Pets that seemed important before baby arrived become utterly unimportant after.

MUMS
AND SCHOOL

School has got a lot harder for mothers. I can't remember my mother getting involved in my homework at all – it wasn't that important. My own children's homework on the other hand has been a serious headache. Once they're past the colouring-in stage (if only you could earn a living by colouring in – I am seriously good at not going over the lines) homework bags start coming through the front door. It's such a downer on family life. Endless homework sheets, times tables charts in their rooms, weekly spelling tests, never mind SATS and reading. Reading books are so dull! It was a struggle to stay awake, listening to the kids read them to me.

The school run didn't even exist until the seventies. You either sent your children to the local school and they walked there with a good raincoat and a satchel, sometimes with friends, and a nice lollipop lady saw them over the difficult bits, or you sent the children away to posh public schools leaving mothers free to organise point-to-points and bark orders at staff.

Mothers must be the bane of teachers' lives. They never just casually stand at the school gates, they are gathering important information about what reading books are in other children's reading folders, or who has been picked for the assembly reading this week, or who has been selected for the Maths project. They gather this information without anyone (other than other mothers) noticing. They might be chatting about the summer fayre, or *Corrie*, or the latest Boden catalogue, but there is a rigorous subtext. Information is being gathered, logged, processed and will be acted on once some further interrogation over tea takes place. So in Maths, does Ben Hardwick always get full marks? Does he get extra different work from Mrs Tippett or does he just do it really quickly? Is Sophie Bennett's mum a supply teacher? Do any of the others in your class seem to know what subjects you are doing on the curriculum already when Mrs Tippett tells you? My children could eventually spot this happening; years of experience told them that I was not just casually interested, I was plotting. Whenever they caught me doing it they would tell me emphatically that I was not allowed to go into school and complain: 'Dad, tell her she is not allowed to say anything to the headmistress.' 'No of course I won't, darling.' (Ooops, did I just say a great big fat fib there?)

Going into school to 'help'

One strategy of surveillance that is open to mothers who can get the time off work is to go into school 'to help'. Maddeningly, some teachers are wise to this, and spiteful headmistresses allocate you to help in a class other than your own child's, which is a bitter blow because you had hoped to be gauging exactly where your child was in the reading stakes, but have to make do with finding out what being on the red table or the yellow table means in the other class, then coming home to ask them what colour theirs is.

But mothers will find stuff out, they just will. I know of no headmistress clever enough to stop this. For a start, dinner time and play time are good surveillance tools. Mothers will find out who are the troublemakers, who has to have a teacher sat next to them at dinner time, and, most importantly, who not to invite back to tea, and definitely who not to invite to the next birthday party. Mothers size other children up in a jiffy. They can do stuff like that. That's because mothers are witches.

The other mothers

Mothers may be experts at fighting their child's corner with the teachers, but they all come up against a roadblock with other mothers. Other mothers are much more tricky than the kids or the teachers, and the most dangerous are mothers with time on their hands. They waft off after the school run and go to pamper days and lunch with the girls and jointly plot fund-raising activities that will get them deep into the heart of the school administration block. They probably have a supply teacher in their midst who is the ring-leader. She has access to some seriously important information – like which exam board the school use, how UCAS points work, and how school projects are marked. She has a dark secret that even the inner sanctum of devious mums don't know about: she writes some of Bethany's projects, she does some of her spelling tests at home, she can even imitate Bethany's handwriting. These mothers are on first-name terms with the school secretary, they might even get themselves on to the PTA. They are therefore in control of lesser mothers.

Yummy Mummies

This is a relatively new category of mum. Their arrival signalled the end of mothers looking like battleaxes. Suddenly at the school gate stand mothers who somehow manage the school run, keep everyone in clean socks, plus a full-time job and still look as though they've spent an hour at the hairdresser's. They go to sports day in heels, they probably run the mum race in a pencil skirt, and they undoubtedly don't have grey-wash underwear or nag their husbands. Most mothers feel that the world would be a better place without the yummy mummy. Bring back mothers who don't ever take their pinny off and are daubed with snot and baby sick, we say. They can still scrub up well when the occasion arises, but let them do the school run in their dog-walking anorak and some seriously comfortable shoes without feeling inferior.

Parents evenings

This is the interface between normal lesser mums and scary other mothers. Clever mothers, usually stay-at-home ones, have parents night sussed – they're the first in the queue for English, and are out and back home and sitting down with a cup of tea when working mothers are only just starting the whole wretched process, unable to work out which teacher to see or which queue to join first.

The problem with parents night for kids is that your mum gets to see other mums too – inevitably ones with a child who behaves better or achieves infinitely more than you do. Your mum will have to listen to scary mum showing off in the queue for each teacher, telling everyone how her eldest daughter's been prematurely accepted to study law at Cambridge.

Mums are desperate to know that their child is doing well. They want to know the mark they got in the exam, but more than anything they want to know where they are ranked in the class, which is naturally classified information. Teachers, however, do not realise that mothers can read upside down. Mums know just where the eye should go to find out where everyone is ranked – it's in the far column on the right, and sometimes clever teachers cover it up with a book, but if you are devious enough (and let's face it, you are – after all, you're a mother) you'll ask them a complicated question about a mark your darling boy got last term which you want to query and while they're turning over the pages the teacher will inadvertently reveal the column with the all-important ranking numbers. Trouble is, sometimes you wish you hadn't found out.

Teachers have had to deal with mums all year. Sometimes they could cheerfully have murdered one or two of the pushier, more interested mums, and at the end of term they get their own back when they write the annual reports, offering advice such as:

* Your child has delusions of adequacy.
* Your son is depriving a village somewhere of an idiot.
* Your son sets low personal standards and then consistently fails to achieve them.
* This child has been working with glue too much.
* When your daughter's IQ reaches fifty, she should sell.
* The gates are down, the lights are flashing, but the train isn't coming.
* If this student were any more stupid, he'd have to be watered twice a week.
* It's impossible to believe the sperm that created this child beat 1,000,000 others.

Dragon Mothers

Recent years have seen the arrival of a new, stricter-than-ever mum on the block – the Dragon Mum. These are the sort of über-strict Chinese mothers (I'm sure 'mum' would never be allowed) who make Venus and Serena Williams look as though they lacked focus.

Dragon Mothers manage to prevent their children from doing anything that might contaminate their minds from the main objective, which is to be obedient and successful. Sleepovers, play dates, watching TV, having pointless hobbies, being in school plays, getting anything less than an A-star in anything at all are not permitted.

Sometimes Dragon Mothers need to get a grip. Worse still, what happens when their kids really do need grounding or get up to the kind of thing normal mothers have to deal with on a regular basis, such as a sleepover involving a twelve-year-old downing a bottle of 70 per cent proof alcohol and being sick all over a Jack Russell cross, or a play date consisting of three hours of crying for their mum and pooing in the Play-Doh?

Fallouts

Mums are forever sorting out squabbles and cliques and fallouts – particularly if they have daughters. The school is useless in such matters, hoping to rise above it by just telling everyone to play nicely. As a result the business of cutting down to size a bossy child has to fall to the mothers. Fallouts that are happening at school are therefore exactly mirrored at the school gates between the mums.

You can always tell if there have been punch-ups between mothers at school: there'll be blood on the pavement. It gets really ugly if one mother decides to give someone else's child a piece of her mind, as in: Chloë would really appreciate it if you didn't ignore her so much at lunch, or I know you keep telling Sophie that your pigtails are longer than hers, but actually your hair is really horrid. The cleverer way to do this is to capture the offending child and get them on your own turf. Clever mothers ask the offending child round to tea after school and pin them against the wall when their own child is not looking, scare them into behaving. Mothers when they are in protection mode are seriously dangerous.

Sizing friends up

So far as my mum was concerned, children's friends always came in two categories:

The nice kids – bland, polite, cardigan-wearing, vegetable-eating

The 'not in my house you're not' kids – at the age of seven already condemned by all-seeing-Mum to a future of drug-dealing/robbery/arson and generally 'leading astray'.

Of course, tension brews when other parents are seen to put your own children in the second category. This becomes WAR. In my case, the parents who did this would eat family meals to the sound of classical music, were deeply religious and had already planned their eight-year-old's medical career. Unfortunately for them, their eldest son always tried to peer through the keyhole when guests were on the toilet. When that came out my mum was very smug and announced, 'Looks like Beethoven doesn't stop little boys from trying to look at vaginas.' It may not be the snappiest catchphrase, but it was appropriate at the time. And of course, it vindicated my mum's worldview. Her child was all right – it's the others you need to worry about.

School trips

School trips are your mother's first test of whether she can manage an entire day without expiring with worry even though you are only going to the Telford Industrial Museum. Some mothers choose to spend the extra free time doing something for themselves, others volunteer to be one of the mums going on the trip 'to help'. Once your child is over the age of six this is a great idea for mothers and a truly terrible idea for the child. There is nothing worse than trying to have a day out with your class mates while your mother looks on/makes sure you get a window seat/is finding stuff out you don't want her to.

School trips which involve overnights are the next test of separation anxiety – not on your part but your mother's. It starts with a Woodcraft camping trip only half an hour down the road but as a mother you have your eye on the weather forecast for weeks before departure, amending your packing list and resolving to drop off some more dry bedding if the weather looks outstandingly dreadful. Turning up unannounced is a truly bad idea, but mothers do it nevertheless – only the once. I could have cheerfully wrung my mother's neck when she arrived at the school camp with some dry underwear, even though (obviously) I badly needed dry underwear. Children and teachers are much happier once they get to senior school, because mums are unwelcome. Frankly, I can see why.

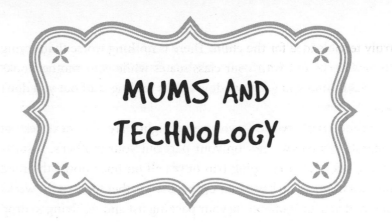

MUMS AND TECHNOLOGY

Mums don't really get technology. It's not that they're stupid, more that their brains are clogged up with other important information like what day the green bins get collected, when the dog needs worming, or remembering to Sky+ *EastEnders*.

They don't have time for technology. OK, so they do have time for Fruit Ninja and Angry Birds, but on the whole they don't have time for technology, and they certainly don't have time to read the manual. They'd rather spend an hour pressing every available button or turning every dial until eventually, after a process of elimination, one of them works. *Anything* rather than sit down to read the manual.

Either that or they enlist someone – usually a teenager – to give them a lesson on how to use their new toy in baby language. When mums get really old and turn into nannas they write basic instructions on how to use their TV remote or their mobile on the back of an old Christmas card. In my mother's case she wrote her own mobile number underlined on such a card next to the word 'ME'. Invariably these instructions make total sense when they are being explained and précised on their piece of card, but make no sense at all a week later. Mums and nannas are therefore seriously high maintenance when it comes to technology. They're bad at owning up that they don't understand. 'Got it,' my mother would say, when she hadn't. 'Oh yes' they say, but then you walk away from them and they tell you they've already forgotten how to turn it on.

Most mothers have just the one technological strategy up their sleeve: turning things off and then on again. If that doesn't work, you need to get the man in, or persuade your daughter's long-term boyfriend to do it.

Mums can rarely be bothered even to read the instructions on food packets. They figure that they've been cooking roast dinners for so long, never mind weighing it and referring to the Delia cooking chart, they bung it in the oven until they think it's done. Mothers – or better still, grandmothers – know if a big lump of pork or turkey is done or not. They just know stuff like that. As if being champion gravy makers they can tell by poking a bit of meat whether it's done, just like they can smell a piece of fish pie and know if it's past its sell-by date. They don't need to read the instructions or the use-by date, because mothers and grandmothers are seriously clever.

Technology is, of course, what Dad is for. So much so it should be written into the wedding vows:

'Do you, Paul, take this woman, Sheila, to solder and to weld, to reboot and to rewire, to defuse and to programme as per the manual instructions from this day forward?'

There is nothing at all about technology that my mum understands. From how to turn on the computer to how to send a text it's all an incomprehensible blur. Every time my kids return home for the weekend we have the same conversation, which goes:

> **'The thingy for the Internet isn't working.'**
> **'What do you mean?'**
> **'The bit that talks to the computer.'**
> **'The router?'**
> **'Yep.'**
> **'Is it switched on?'**
> **'Erm …'**

Most mothers need help with the following:

- ❀ Re-tuning the TV in her bedroom
- ❀ Making the DVD player 'talk to' the TV. She can't work the DVD player, but then she doesn't really want to because it involves getting down on the floor.
- ❀ Changing the time on her alarm clock
- ❀ Resetting the microwave so it isn't permanently on defrost
- ❀ 'Mending' the TV remote (which involves telling her to point the remote, not her mobile, at the TV in future)

One mum was asked at work if there was power point available in a meeting room, to which her answer was yes, as far as she could remember there were lots of plug sockets.

And why do mums constantly ask how to update their iPods? For the thousandth time, you just plug it into your laptop.

Mums think lol means lots of love and not laugh out loud. So they get confused when you put lol in the middle of a message.

> One of my closest friends went on holiday with her mum as a girly treat after her mum and dad had separated. Her mum was enjoying some of the attention from the local barmen and, seeing no harm in it, my friend had a chuckle as she tried to engage in a little cross-cultural flirting. However, the situation turned a little sour later on and my friend's mum stormed back to her, having slapped the man across the face.
>
> 'What's wrong?' my friend asked, concerned.
>
> 'He's sick,' her mum replied. 'He got out his phone and said he wants to SMS me. I'm not into all that kinky shit.'

MOTHERS CAN ALSO BE EMBARRASSINGLY SLOW, AS EXEMPLIFIED BY THIS TEXT FROM MUM:

MuM: KUM

ME: um … what?

MuM: u no. key under mat. every1 nos that 1.

SURFING
MUMS

others do spend a lot of time at the computer, what do they spend their time doing? Take a look at some of their Google search histories:

- ❀ How old is Lulu?
- ❀ Sleep clinics
- ❀ Arrivals board Heathrow/JFK
- ❀ *Daily Mail* online
- ❀ Jo Malone
- ❀ Plumbers
- ❀ Orthodontists
- ❀ What is female Viagra?
- ❀ eBay
- ❀ QVC
- ❀ QVC
- ❀ John Lewis direct
- ❀ Facebook
- ❀ Swimming costumes that pull you in
- ❀ How to remove candlewax from a tablecloth
- ❀ QVC
- ❀ Signs of breast cancer
- ❀ Facebook

- ✿ Why do men have nipples?
- ✿ Why do men cheat?
- ✿ Is my to-do list killing my sex life?
- ✿ Why is my goldfish not eating?
- ✿ How do I explain sex to my kids without making them want to do it?
- ✿ Are all teenagers evil?
- ✿ Does female Viagra work?
- ✿ Can I stop menopause symptoms?
- ✿ How to lose weight quickly
- ✿ How to lose weight quicker
- ✿ How do I find out what my daughter has looked at on the Internet / How to erase research history [by far the favourite search]

TEXTS MUMS SEND

TEXTS MUMS SEND ARE IN A CLASS OF THEIR OWN TOO. SUCH AS:

Granddad taken to hospital. Put tea on mumx

Are you home yet?

Text me when you set off

Text me when you get there

Are you sure you used plain flour?

Don't forget Dad's birthday

* * *

Mum text to daughter: Your dad and I are getting divorced

Daughter: What … … … … … … … !!!!!!!!!!!!!!!!!!!!!!!

Mum text to daughter: Your phone is working then

* * *

* * *

MUM who is on diet to daughter who is downstairs: Plz can you bring me a sandwich to my room. Don't tell anyone, please don't say anything to your dad.

* * *

MUM: Hi love, good luck for today. Me and Dad just wanted you to check on the weather conditions because someone said that the pavement was icy where you are and we are worried that you might not have the right shoes. Your dad wants me to tell you that he fell over on the ice. Lots of love.

* * *

MUM: Your great aunt just passed away, LOL.
DAUGHTER: Why is that funny?
MUM: It's not funny, what do you mean?
DAUGHTER: LOL means laughing out loud.
MUM: Oh my goodness, I thought it meant lots of love. I sent that to everyone. I'll have to call everyone back!!!

* * *

My own spectacular technophobic trick is that I got myself a Canadian email address by mistake – something which I couldn't repeat if my life depended on it – and now when I log on it tells me the weather and latest news in Ottawa and sends me ads for restaurants in Montreal. It's a marvellous feeling that they are all wasting their time on me.

MUMS AND CARS

If you ask me what sort of car I drive my first thought would be it's black. As long as I can find it in a car park and I know which sort of petrol to put in it, that's as much as I need to know. It would be much more helpful in garage showrooms just to group them in colours rather than drone on about model descriptions: as in, red cars black cars or silver cars.

Fancy car technology is wasted on me. I used to have a four-wheel drive but didn't have the courage to ever put it into four-wheel drive because it involved another diddy gear stick and I was warned – oh so warned – that if you didn't remember to do something or other when you used the diddy gear stick then the whole engine would grind to a halt or the whole world as I knew it would come to an end. I knew that in the terror of the moment I would be bound to get it wrong, so I spent two really bad winters sliding up and down the hill into town from our house in a car that weighed about two tons and was probably more dangerous than a normal car in ordinary-wheel drive.

I'm ashamed to say I don't even really understand the steering-into-a-skid rule. People have explained it to me, but it makes no sense at all. If I was in a skid I would truly have no idea which way to turn the wheel. All I know is that if you turn it one way it makes the skid a whole lot worse. Sadly, I don't know which way that is.

So mums, despite the fact that we are laden down with worry and anxiety, are a bit crap in a car-related crisis.

And if there had been a parking test when I took my driving test I would still have the L plates on today.

I can't work lawnmowers, or drills, or DVD cameras, or screenwash fillers, or check tyre pressures or operate DIY equipment of any kind. All I can do is work my mobile, the Internet and eBay. That's about it. And they say men are good at being bad at things they don't want to do! Mothers, I suspect, are much much better at that.

It's not just complicated technology most mothers can't do. Have you ever watched a mother in a rowing boat? I am physically incapable of working out which way to put my oar in to make the boat go the way I want it to go. I get it wrong every single time. In fact, I am special needs when it comes to rowing boats.

INVENTIONS MOTHERS WOULD WELCOME

A nice Hoover that doesn't weigh a ton

Anti-wrinkle cream that does what it says on the jar

A computer that behaves itself and doesn't have sulks or is spiteful

An onion chopper that just gets on with it so that your mascara wouldn't run, and then doesn't require cleaning by hand

One size tights that fit

A seriously good automatic ironing machine that you just load the stuff in and it comes out on hangers with some nice smelly starch spray on (but this would have to be our little secret since having to do the ironing is a big big plus when you want to get your own way with something else or send the old man out in a blizzard to buy chocolate from the garage at night)

137

A dishwasher that doesn't need unloading

A lie detector that would fit snugly on a kitchen worktop

A pill which means you can eat kettle crisps and not take in a single calorie

A dry white wine bottle that always looks two-thirds full despite the fact that you've had a <u>third</u> glass most nights this week

Easily the best invention for mothers for centuries: the epidural. At last, a truly useful invention.

YOU'LL NEED A COAT

lothes are a big source of conflict for mothers and children. It's all about control. You had it and you didn't. She spent years dressing you the way she wanted to, putting your hair in pigtails and making you wear Start-rite sandals. Possibly even over white ankle socks. She even made you go to big school in short trousers – and you have the photos to prove it. There is a picture of me at about four as a bridesmaid for my Aunty Doreen. It had a touch of the big fat gypsy wedding about it – the dress, not the wedding, I hasten to add. I can still feel the horrible scratchy synthetic netting underneath it and the frankly silly headdress that meant I couldn't tear up and down the dance floor without it falling off. My mother loved it. I think she cried a bit when I put it on. I thought it was hideous. Even at four I knew this dress was wrong, and that I had no choice in the matter. I – like all children – stored this resentment up for future reference.

Clothes are particularly tricky for mothers and daughters, which is a complicated relationship to start with. They don't just rub along effortlessly, they veer from being joined at the hip, I-know-what-she's-thinking one minute, to putting the knife in just where it hurts most the next. And often clothes are involved. Clothes are the no-go zones, the hard-helmet areas of everyday conflict that can lead to some seriously bad behaviour on both sides, ranging from flouncing off in a strop in a shopping centre, to full-on hand-on-hip screaming matches that would scare the neighbours, with a drizzle of serious sulking for good measure. These areas of conflict between mothers and daughters never let up, yet it's not as if they are earth-shatteringly important, when you think about it. Typically, they boil down to three things: clothes, hair and shoes.

Actually, I've just thought about it, and these are shatteringly important issues.

When you're little, mums can basically do what they like on the clothes front. If my mother didn't like something of mine, or indeed of my father's, she'd just move it to somewhere we'd never find it. Her favourite hiding places were jammed behind the hot-water tank in the airing cupboard, or on top of a wardrobe – but so far back you'd have to get on a step ladder to find it. It was her way of preventing me or my father wearing things we liked and she hated. My father was unbelievably patient with her; she pretty much shopped for all his clothes while he acquiesced for the sake of a quiet life. There was just one piece of clothing he drew the line at being forbidden to wear – his beloved anorak. Which she took to the charity shop and he bought back at least twice to my knowledge.

With daughters it starts well. All little girls want to look like their mothers – except my girls wanted to look like me, but a much more glamorous version of me – presumably because I spent the whole time at home in jeans and a pinny. They would plead with me to wear ball gowns (like I ever went to a ball!) and in desperation Ellen painted me at nursery with my ball gown going round the supermarket, which was her way of saying, 'Raise your game, lady.' Already she knew she didn't like my style.

As daughters we are genetically programmed to rebel against our mother's taste in fashion. It's our way of expressing our need to be individuals. My mother liked things with a nice collar, as she'd put it, or a neck. And she was obsessed with matching. In fact, her matching didn't stop at clothes; we had so many matching

soft furnishings in our lounge that it was hard to find anything or anyone with all the matching items acting effectively as camouflage.

I was concerned about how my mother dressed, not because I thought she should look more gorgeous – don't be absurd! No, as a child you are desperate for your mother not to stand out, because if she stands out then people will notice her and you don't want that, God no, because she defines who *you* are. One look at her and everyone has sized you up in a second. Some people are unfortunate enough to have mothers who dress to be noticed – big hats, big shoes, big fashion statements – and my heart bleeds for them.

Recently my two daughters made me have a massive clear-out of clothes, accusing me of wearing baggy big tops to cover my midriff and saying that I should make more of my bust and waistline, a result of them spending hours in front of *Britain's Top Model* and Gok Wan. They both sat on the bed while I took all my clothes out one by one and voted them in or out. Needless to say, all my waterfall cardigans and Per Una numbers didn't even get fully held up before they were consigned to the reject pile with yuks and ohmigods. They had an absolute ball, bonding in sisterly hatred of their mother's image. It took a whole car to get the reject pile to the charity shop, leaving me with a very modest number of outfits. I was told by them to buy a lot of belted jackets or pull in tops at the waist and wear heels more. It's all right for them, all they have to worry about is a touch of visible panty line. (Obviously I have since bought a lot of new waterfall cardigans and Per Una.)

The other problem is the amount of clothes. Mum's are *obsessed* with dressing their children for the weather, although I've no idea why they bother; the time will come when their daughters will wear a miniskirt clubbing even in a snowdrift. Mothers do go a bit over the top at the first sign of snow, insisting on tights, polo neck, sweat pants, long socks, gloves, a hat, a scarf, a snow suit, and a winter coat – just to play in small amounts of snow. Most children can hardly move their limbs.

I see the vest as a landmark in mother/daughter communication. The moment the daughter questions the validity of the vest as an item of clothing, that bond of unshakeable trust in Mum's judgement has been broken. When your kids are little you can send them to school all snuggled up with a pair of mittens on a string up their coat sleeves, prepared as you would want them to be for all weather eventualities but looking as if they have just run amok in lost property and are wearing everything they could find. They don't have a lot of choice, other than to leave it all in lost property, which clever kids probably do. The trouble starts when they get older.

The clothes battle between mothers and daughters revs up at senior school. Your mother sends you for your first day of term with your new satchel, your skirt with bulky hem with room for growth and, crucially, a coat. Coats as far as kids are concerned are only for geeks, and even if children do wear coats, once they get to senior school they don't on principle ever do them up. Even though the sun is shining – it's early September – your mother insists on you taking a coat ... as she will every day of your life till you are in your forties. But you get to school and no one else is wearing coats. The first thing I said to my mother when she picked me up from my first big day at secondary school was, 'NO ONE WAS WEARING COATS!' I was furious with her, knowing that my credibility had been ruined and clawing back any self-esteem from this saddo image was going to take me ages. Spookily, exactly the same pattern was repeated when my eldest went to senior school. And it wasn't until she came out of the school gates looking furious and dragging her coat on the floor in disdain that I realised history had repeated itself. From then on it's full-on war, because she's found you out, she knows you don't always get it right.

Stupid shoes

As a mother, I confess I judge people a little on their shoes. Shoes, like nothing else, are barometers of wholesomeness or otherwise. So it was a sad day when my children refused to wear their Start-rites – the black patent party ones, or the bright red leather ones, or the brown leather sandals with aerated patterns on the top. That was just the start of the punch-ups. Sandals except for flip-flops have become no-gos for both my daughters, they are to be avoided at all costs since, as far as they're concerned, only saddos wear sandals. Footwear for them has to be high (ridiculously high) heels, ballet pumps or flip-flops. In short, they will only wear stupid shoes. That's it. Any other structural shoe of any sort is a no-no; wellies, sturdy boots or anything practical are laughably sad. They come home with sopping wet feet or blisters that never heal after partying all night and somehow the sense, the logic in either changing a shoe when you get somewhere or sensible shoes is like a foreign language for them. They just don't get it.

Naturally before I was a mother I loved stupid shoes too and my own mother's strategy was either to hide, or in extreme cases destroy shoes she disapproved of when I wasn't looking. I came home from a school trip in Germany when I was thirteen with a pair of red patent stack-heeled sling-back shoes that I had invested my spending money in, aware subconsciously that this was my way of making it clear that, once home, I was *so* not going to be a little girl any longer but a Slade rock queen like the common girls at the secondary modern. She said she was worried about me breaking my ankle in them (nice try with the health-and-safety route), but the look of disdain when I wore them was almost like a bad smell in the air. She knew exactly why I loved them. They screamed 'Take me, I'm yours' to all the boys.

First she'd move them so that just as I was getting ready to go out to my first discos I couldn't find them; claiming, as ever, that she hadn't touched them. Then it was full-on warfare between us. Eventually I found them in the dustbin when she had had a 'clear-out'. My father got involved in that one it was so serious and it backfired horribly on her. I never entirely trusted her again. But it goes to show the lengths that some mothers will go to to protect their daughter's honour. Looking back, they were absurdly tarty. And she knew it.

You're not going out looking like that

Oh yes – and who's going to stop me then?

One of the most damaging phrases in a mother–daughter relationship is: 'But so-and-so's mum lets her.' This can be the reasoning behind a multitude of fashion aberrations – most memorably the phase when it was fashionable to show a diamanté-covered thong over the top of your jeans. Of course, all girls worth their salt knew to leave the house as Mum intended and change at your best friend's before the disco.

Mums these days have more to deal with than just miniskirts. Instead of worrying simply that they might catch a chill in their lady-bits, now mums could equally end up with girls who are Goths or emos. The kids might actually be having the last laugh though. I saw a girl who was about sixteen on a bus wearing heavy make-up, a mini dress, ripped tights with bright 'barbie' blonde hair. She said to her friend, 'I don't really like dressing like this, but it stops my parents from dragging me everywhere with them.'

Shopping for clothes with your mother

It's a recipe for disaster. As a mother, you go hoping for a bonding experience like those mothers and daughters you see walking arm in arm in shopping centres. As a daughter, you go along with it, but only because Mum has the credit card.

For a start you both want to go to different shops. My daughters will not, on principle, shop in Clarks or M&S as they see both those shops as mum shops. If I am ever stupid enough to buy them clothes for their birthday, the first question is: Where did it come from? On the basis that, if they liked it, and if it did come from either of those two shops, they would have lost the battle. The second question is: Did you keep the receipt?

Shopping for clothes with your daughter involves traipsing round for hours in shops that are staffed by people for whom the answer to every single question is 'Everything's out'. You lose the will to live in Topshop and eventually just give in and buy anything so you can go home, having spent over an hour on a stupid little stool someone begrudgingly brings you in the changing-room corridor. The moment you pick something out and say the dreaded words, 'You'd look lovely in that, darling' – normally something in navy, or what you would call smart, or involving polka dots – they don't even bother to look up before saying 'Yuk! God, Mum, what are you thinking of!' or 'You mean for YOU???'

Clearly, reverse logic is the way to go; so you pick up the things you think are hideous and say, 'You'd look lovely in that, darling!' This double bluff has worked a couple of times, putting them off buying some ghastly clingy cheap revealing top ... but sadly they are now wise to it.

The other thing that they don't get with clothes is questions like 'But what will it go with?' Nothing goes, you moron! they think, or say out loud. Nothing matters as in matching or going with, you just jumble the whole thing up. The less it matches, the more they like it. Nothing anyone wears in Topshop goes with anything – that's the point. Once again, history is repeating itself. I am becoming my own mother in response to my daughters becoming the old me. It's God's way of telling us that you are now officially being handed the genetic baton.

Having fun shopping with mummy.
Bethan McGregor Age 6

Tattoos and body piercing

Some mothers have to deal with bigger issues than short skirts and high heels, and quite a lot of them, judging by the fact that the whole world has gone tattoo crazy. In our small market town alone there are two tattoo shops, which I could cheerfully letter bomb since they are encouraging kids to have tattoos that they are going to regret later in life. Ditto body piercing. But what can you do? As a mother, the more fuss you make about it and the more abhorrent you find it, the more likely they are to go ahead and do it. The best way to discourage these 'adornments' is either to keep shtum or have something done yourself – a major deterrent. After all, sometimes motherhood involves sacrifices. That's what my mother should have done with those red shoes – if she had borrowed them and worn them into town herself, I'd never have worn them again.

Hair

Mothers control your hair for as long as they can. Even when you're old enough to talk to the hairdresser yourself about what you want done, your mother is entirely capable of having a quiet word with her while you're reading your *Blue Peter* annual to say she wants plenty off the bottom to save coming back too soon. With hideous and life-changing results in my case. Hey presto, I walked out looking like Peter Pan in an A-line skirt.

The conflict lasts well into old age. I remember my mother nagging her own mother about having a perm when her hair had obviously been permed so much that it was more like acrylic loft lagging than real hair. Every Sunday we'd go round for roast dinner and the first thing my mother would say was, 'Have you had your hair permed again?' Accusatory, pulling at it even, and her mother would say, 'I had to – it looks awful otherwise.' I used to feel so

My mother had a habit of giving me a quiff which is visible in all my baby photos – presumably she had been at my father's Brylcreem.

sorry for her. Alas, once my own mother got to the stage of her hair being so frizzy and thin it no longer looked like hair I would give her a really hard time about it. Too mean to go to the hairdresser's and have highlights or proper colour, she'd use those DIY wash-out ones, leaving a hideous mess on the sink and her hair an unfeasible colour. I don't know why she just didn't let it all go grey, I thought. On and on I'd go about her hair and how she should do it differently; she'd pretend to listen, then just go back to her usual: a shampoo and set and home-made hair dye. Now I am in my fifties my hair has spitefully started to go like hers: greying, thinning – no one warned me about that – and hideously frizzy. And guess what: I have invested in a set of hair rollers. Somehow they pull out the frizz like nothing else does. Although I am not about to have a shampoo and set, I can suddenly see the logic of the way my mother, and my mother's mother did their hair and why they resorted to perms. Oh, the shame – and I was so horrid about it.

MIND HOW YOU GO

others spend their whole lives worrying in case Something Happens to their children. A mother's love is the most powerful thing I have ever experienced, both giving it and receiving it. It trumps everything. Walks on the beach, nice piles of newly ironed laundry, a newly made bed, a lovely sunset, swimming in the sea … Nothing comes close – and it's not until you experience it that you can grasp that.

The stakes are therefore so high it's no wonder we almost expire with anxiety once we are a mother. I remember with my first-born thinking, Well, if she can just get to her first birthday, or if I can buy her a party dress with a big sash bow to tie and some shiny black party shoes, I'll be happy. Maybe God you could just grant me that for now, that'll keep me going … Which was bizarre, looking back, given how much she looked like Ross Kemp in a toupee when she was born.

'Mind how you go.' What a pointless saying that is, and yet my mother probably said it to me every single time I went out of the front door. Which is just as well, because unless she had I probably wouldn't have bothered looking before I crossed the road at all, or I might have driven the wrong way down the dual carriageway because it slipped my mind, or sky-dived from the top of the office building just for the hell of it. *Not*. But saying it made her feel better, like touching wood or crossing your fingers behind your back – and of course I find myself saying it too. My mother would say that if she could have wrapped me up in cotton wool to keep me safe, she would have done. Maybe that's why she sent me to school in coats that made me look like a lagged boiler.

As a mother you are on constant alert for hazards such as choking, falling, tripping, electrocution or straightforward escape. Nothing, absolutely nothing, prepares you for how utterly worrying the whole process is from beginning to end. I overheard a mother recently whose small children were running on the pavement. 'Stop running,' she told them: 'I saw several children trip on this kerb and break their ankles recently, and I bet it would really hurt.' You see what she did there? I'm sorry, but I am not sure that tripping on a kerb is so dangerous that she would have seen more than one child break their ankle that way, and then she had to top it off with 'and it would really hurt'. Still, it stopped them running. Frankly, they weren't really in any danger at all – but then they weren't my children, you see, so it doesn't count.

The stakes couldn't be any higher and it explains why, for mothers, worrying is a full-time job. The rest of their lives have to fit in around the worrying, including their actual job. On some level or other, whether we are in a meeting, on the other side of the world or even asleep, mothers are worrying. The worry list is constantly ticking over, processing all the possible disasters that could befall their children, like a computer constantly scanning for viruses. Until eventually – often at three in the morning – a hideously worrying idea takes shape and thrusts itself to the top of the list. It's like an air traffic control centre womaned twenty-four hours a day, looking out for potential enemy aircraft.

My worry list is constantly changing. One minute it's a daughter mentioning that she has a tummy ache, the next I'm worrying she's spending far too much time on her computer … And right at the top of the worry pile is something seriously scary like the holiday with her friends straight after A levels in Zante for a week. I had never even heard of Zante. Initially I was impressed, imagining they might be going to look at Ancient Greek ruins. However, mention Zante to anyone with teenage children and the reaction is always the same: Oh my God you will be so relieved when she comes back! She got back in one piece, but only after one girl fell over drunk the night they got there and broke her wrist, and the other one missed her period and spent the whole time doing pregnancy tests and throwing up – even before the vodka. Playing Florence Nightingale to her friends might have been a hideous drag, but at least it kept my own daughter out of further trouble.

What can you do? As a mother, the more you warn them not to do something the more – if you're not careful – you give them the idea that it might be seriously interesting. No, the only sensible strategy when they're teenagers is to keep them short of money.

Even when they're home from uni, you worry. They don't answer a text and your instant reaction is: Are they OK? Might they have fallen down the stairs? Will they have left the grill on and gone back to bed? What if, what if, what if …?

Most of us become Helicopter Mums once they've left home – forever hovering in case there is an emergency. Ellen has just gone to Thailand on her gap trip. I kept asking her if she needed a visa. 'They haven't said so,' was her answer. 'Yes, but have you checked?' was my response. A week before she left, I asked her again: 'Have you checked whether you need a visa?' Same answer. So of course Helicopter Mum goes on the website and yes, she does need a visa. There is nothing like a Helicopter Mum in action – within an hour I had arranged to get it to London and processed and picked up between my meetings. Job done. Crisis averted. I know I shouldn't. I know I should leave her to make her own mistakes, but her little face was so relieved, and that is mum heaven.

The Gap is challenging for mums. Most of us worry ourselves into an early grave when they're backpacking in the Third World.

We've never watched the news so studiously in our lives for evidence of calamities on the other side of the world. We see them off, come home and track the flight, logging on to check the Arrivals board in Bangkok and flicking between that and Sky breaking news. From then on we're on red alert 24/7. We've seen the itinerary, it has words like 'remote', 'basic', 'malaria', 'precautionary', and the dreaded 'rafting'. We count down the days till they come home. We live for their texts to prove they are still alive. I Skyped Ellen recently in Thailand and she wanted me to point the camera into the fridge, which was her way of saying she was homesick. I'm homesick for her. We cry when we go to Arrivals at Heathrow to pick them up, and then cry some more in the car on the way home. Then guess what: the moment they're home and you've got the first wash on, they announce that they're going out to meet their mates at the pub to tell them all about it.

Even when the children leave home, mothers continue to worry like no one else. The only good thing about kids leaving home is that you no longer know accurately what they might be up to, so your worrying is rather ill-thought through, out of date, irrelevant and as such a bit more likely to be solved by a pep talk or a don't be so silly talk from a supportive husband. It doesn't necessarily mean there is nothing to worry about (alas), but more that your worries are inaccurate. You think they might be out clubbing but they are actually early to bed because they are going bungee jumping in the morning. All you can hope for is that they tell you about the bungee jump when they've done it, and with luck not from an A&E department.

People say that you never stop worrying about your children and this is true. If it's not whether they'll poke their fingers into plug sockets, it'll be who's being horrid to them in the playground, whether their temperature has come down, or if they have got home from clubbing at three in the morning – and that's before they've even learned to drive. Women say that they continue worrying until their dying day. Great. Interestingly, when my mother was a full-time mum there were no childproof lids on medicine bottles, no baby locks on kitchen cupboards, kids played in the street, there were no seat belts, nut allergies were unheard of, pools were unsupervised, risks were never assessed ... and yet somehow most of us survived.

Because mothers are full-time worriers they can't afford to let their guard down for a moment, which means that just about everything they ever say is part of a sophisticated constant agenda. Talking to my mother was like being in a constant but badly chaired meeting. Mothers, like politicians, *always* speak with their agenda in mind. Don't be fooled into thinking she's just engaging in idle chit-chat with you; it's all designed to make a point. The tell-tale sentences often start with 'By the way, I've been meaning to tell you' – they invariably couch their agenda in a casual tone, while busying themselves with some washing up or towel-folding to lull you into a false sense of security – then comes the big point of it all: 'By the way, I've been meaning to tell you: your cousin Victoria has a friend who's being stalked by someone on the Internet. Apparently they traced her through her Facebook profile and invited her to meet. The police got involved – it's all over the local papers. Just goes to show ...' And with that she flounces off nonchalantly. As if to say, Put that in your pipe and smoke it!

Mothers in worry-mode are a force to be reckoned with. They're either cutting articles out of the *Daily Mail* and putting them on their children's bedside table, or posting them to them, or they drop things into the conversation that they think we need to know. Equally, if they suddenly think of something new that could go wrong, they'll be consumed by the need to get this new and therefore urgent worry to you immediately. Typically, mothers can't wait to ask you a question or raise something that's on their mind, and are incapable of holding it in. My mother could never sit down to a family lunch if something that might be harmful to us was on her mind. 'You're not taking drugs, are you?' 'You wouldn't do something stupid, like accept a lift from a minicab without a licence, would you?' she'd demand. And only when the answer was no would she calm down.

As a mother you know it's wrong, but the trouble is you have become a member of the SAS with a liking for occasional tables and comfy shoes. Like a sniffer dog, you are trained to sniff out trouble.

My own anxiety is shamefully bad. When we flew with our eldest for the first time I packed her water rings in the hand luggage just in case we came down on water and there was no time to find her a floating cot. Which I imagine either don't exist or someone has moved in favour of some duty-free goods. That's the level of my anxiety about my children. Bad. I don't know what's worse: the meningitis-watch years or the have-they-come-home-from-the-party-yet? years. Both are exhausting if you are a worrier, which all mums are. And both have given me some seriously deep wrinkles.

And then there are the times you worry yourself to death because they tell you something that is upsetting them, so you spend your day planning a campaign to deal with it, only for them to come home barely able to remember the problem. It's in our DNA, worrying.

Sadly, your children won't thank you for it. *Au contraire*, in fact. Sometimes I find myself looking at my girls, inspecting them for evidence of unhappiness, disease, or malaise, but it's as if they can feel my gaze on them like a laser hitting an ultra-sensitive surface:

'WHAT?' they say. 'Stop looking at me.'

'I'm not looking at you.'

'Yes, you are.'

'I was just wondering how you are.'

'God, you're sad.'

SNOOPING

nooping is a natural by-product of anxiety. Unfortunately, mothers are prone to resort to snooping for evidence of yet further things to worry about. It's not that we want to know any juicy details (at all) of sexual encounters or drunken binges, rather we want to know what we need to worry about.

Obviously mothers don't want to get a reputation for nosiness or snooping. This kind of despicable behaviour, they would argue, is confined to those other mothers for whom they have no respect. Kind of. No, we're cleverer than that … And it doesn't take long to work out that the perfect cover for snooping into your child's life is cleaning and tidying. Like the cleaner who wheels one of those trolleys round hospital or office corridors and is invisible to most, yet knows all there is to know about everybody – how they keep their loose change in top drawers and how to open the biscuit tin without leaving a trail of evidence – mothers are the same. They are the crème de la crème of snoopers, the top brass. Because if you're cleaning you can coast round the house and get into all the little nooks and crannies. Better still, you can do it while they're out. After all, their room has 'got to be cleaned sometime'.

When you're little you don't notice that your room has been cleaned and tidied, not unless she does something gobsmackingly thoughtless like my mother once did. My mother was forever cleaning, sometimes in inverted commas but most of the time not in inverted commas and, thinking he was a bit dirty, she took it upon herself to put my teddy bear in the washing machine. I came home to find him on the Aga drying out, but instead of sitting up to greet me the washing machine had flattened him – looking back, I think she might have resorted to putting him through the wringer. He spent the rest of his life looking like a lumpy omelette and I spent the rest of my life being bitterly angry with her for doing it. I still have the lumpy omelette.

When you're nine you get your first secret diary with a lock on and write down all the things you hate about Melanie Potter and the way she always says she's your best friend then sits next to Jessica Waters at break leaving you looking like Johnny-no-mates. You use the key for the first few days, but from then on you can't be bothered and leave it unlocked. Your mother can now see your innermost thoughts – and you are too young to spot the symmetry between what you are writing in the secret book and the kind of questions your mother is asking or the actions she's taking. As in, 'Are you sure you want to invite Melanie Potter to your sleepover?'

By the time you're a teenager, your bedroom defines you. The vile puce-pink emulsion you make your parents paint it, the posters, the music and eventually the trail of rancid coffee mugs, make-up, then vodka screams: I'm an adult now, so get over it. You probably have KEEP OUT notices on the door, saying ENTER AT YOUR OWN RISK, you might even persuade your parents to have a bolt on the inside. But there are very few households who agree to a lock on the outside. It's called moving out, and until you do so in your absence your room is open to snooping activity big time.

You don't mind her tidying and cleaning your room sometimes – after all, what else has she got to do? – and the first time it happens it's wonderful: you're suddenly in a world of clean sheets, folded laundry and your shoes are all pointing the right way. If she's so sad she wants to spend an entire morning tidying your crap, then let her – or so you think. Then quick as a flash you remember the stuff you'd put under the bed, stuff you didn't want her to see: that stupid letter from pervy Eric, or the magazine article about how to please your man in bed, or God forbid anything with a battery. You remember that the lock on your pretty secret diary isn't that difficult to break; you can't remember where you saw it last, but the jaunty angle it now sits at on your bedside table seems to say, 'Gosh – me? No, I haven't read it, I'm not that sort of mother! I'm fragrant, I have better things to do.' Wrong. No mother has better things to do. No mother (I know) can resist having a sneaky look, and then a sneaky look leads to a full-on bring-up-a-cup-of tea-and-sit-down look, checking for references to drugs, casual sex, or times you've been having so much fun you might have forgotten to look both ways while crossing the road. To draw too much attention to it would be – you realise – foolish, but little by little over the coming weeks evidence trickles out. She asks you tell-tale questions that can only mean she has read it cover to cover: 'David, the one with the yellow mini – is he a safe driver then?' 'When you drove to Brighton that weekend with the girls, did you all have a seat belt in the back?' 'And what do you make of this awful new prevalence of chlamydia?' It's all adding up. She's been snooping.

The best advice to teenagers whose mothers are reading their diary is not to let on but to stuff it full of the most troubling things imaginable … Pregnancy scares, drug dealers, shop-lifting prosecutions, the lot, and just enjoy seeing the blood drain away from her face on a daily basis.

Everyone knows the worst thing you can find in your mum's room is anything to do with the S word. Despite the fact that all of us are the product of our parents' sex lives, we seem internally programmed to deny its existence. My worst experience was helping to move house when I was thirteen and discovering 'the stash' in the loft, which included a board game called 'How's Your Father'. Frankly, in that context, I didn't want to know.

But mums are equally shocked when daughter reaches 'that age'. A friend with a sense of humour that plumbed the depths of depravity gave me a Christmas present and insisted I open it in front of the whole family. It turned out to be a vibrator shaped like a giant banana-shaped stick of rock, to which my nan responded, 'She'll never fit all that in her mouth.' We didn't try to explain.

Facebook stalking is the latest mum-snooping tool. In a moment of weakness you show her how to use Facebook, and the next thing you know she is pasting messages on your wall. Trouble is, she thinks her messages are just to you instead of going to your entire circle of friends. Worse, she doesn't understand how to stop. In fact, someone has founded POOF – get Parents Off Of Facebook. After all, who wants their Facebook covered in messages from their mother telling them about The Change, and reminding them to change their sheets more often?

Actual stalking

Some mums resort to actual stalking. Not virtually, actually. I cannot be the only mother who, dodging behind lampposts all the way, followed their child to school on their first walk alone to check they were all right. Let's face it, if schools made CCTV in the classroom and playground available to parents, mums would get nothing done. In fact they'd woman it 24/7 and plan a shift share.

You snooping in her things

It can work the other way too. Your parents have gone to a nice stately home for the day with your younger brother; they asked you to come as it was a nice sunny day but churlishly you declined saying it was 'a bit windy'. That made you feel good, but then come lunchtime when you're dipping Cheerios in a Cup-a-Soup and watching *Location Location*, something comes over you. What do your parents get up to when no one is looking? You don't really want to know, but then again because you might be able to find out, you think you might as well have a go. You start with the wardrobe shelves, investigate one or two you've never seen your mother go to – and find vinyl collections, tragic RSC programmes from their youth, or some cute baby memorabilia. God, parents are sad. You move on to the drawers: layer after layer of big knickers and baggy Y-fronts, with the odd comfy pair of elasticated trousers, pull-in and push-out underwear that truly takes your breath away and has you making a bargain with yourself to never, ever let yourself go to that extent. No way will you ever need bras that involve civil engineering, with so many hooks and eyes she must feel like Houdini. Nor would you stoop to those nasty nasty whites that have gone a shade of bluey grey – shameful, absolutely shameful! No one would ever fancy her, you think.

Then your hand goes right to the back – hey, it's not even 2 p.m., they'll be looking round some tragic farm shop or picking blackberries – and there's a seriously corsetty looking item. Black. You pull it out. To your horror – and like the moment in *Alien* when the head pops out and scares you to death – you find it has suspenders and no crotch. You trying not to be sick as your world goes into spin and you get a bit dizzy. The woman you thought too old and fat and wobbly to have had sex more than, say, four times (you have a younger brother) and, say, one drunken New Year's Eve and their wedding night … ACTUALLY has a sex life.

You're still my little baby

We have to forgive mothers for their worrying. Despite all evidence to the contrary, mothers always think their children have a mental age of four.

No matter how old you both are – you might both be old enough to draw a pension – to your mum you will always be her baby.

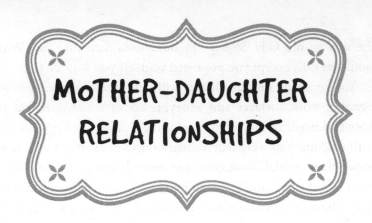

MOTHER–DAUGHTER RELATIONSHIPS

There's something about the mother–daughter relationship which is particularly tricky. Looking at your mother is like looking in a mirror with some nasty smears on it: you look at her and see a reflection of yourself, you see her flaws in you, and yours in her. There's so much history, whether it's the way she used to try to make friends for you on holiday (even when you were seventeen!) or stood at the window to check you had got home safely, or would embellish stories, or could read your mind, or the way she clicks her nails against one another when you're driving … It's the classic case of familiarity breeding contempt. Worse, you can't yell and scream and swear at your mother like you would your partner, because mums go all hurt and huffy, and then you feel more wretched than you ever thought possible.

Turning into your mother

One minute she's getting the sand from between your toes after a day on the beach, and the next minute the roles are reversed and she's sending you into town to pick up her prescription. You see a photo of your mother when you were little and realise that you are now older than she was in that photo, and at the time you thought she was an old lady. Slowly but surely you turn into her. Which would be OK, except you promised yourself you wouldn't.

You've spent decades living with her stupid obsession with cleaning work surfaces and worrying about whether it will rain later and needing to keep on top of the ironing, and it's filled you with disdain. You were determined to do things differently, to rise above these trivial obsessions and busy yourself with matters of more significance and import. She knew different. Like she always does. She pointed out (enjoyed pointing it out) that you would turn into her. She chose her moment to rub it in – perhaps it was on a day when you'd been particularly spiteful to her, maybe you had withheld your latest news when she needed it most or accidentally on purpose forgotten to ring home. You remember her telling you: 'One day you will understand, one day you will know how I feel.' Or, if you'd been particularly foul: 'One day, my girl, you'll regret this, because one day you will know what it's like to be old.'

And guess what. She's right.

This metamorphosis from daughter to mother *will* happen. It is genetically programmed. You too will find it hard to remember people's names, and write your pin number down at the back of your diary. This is all part of God's plan. Passing on the genetic baton. His way of ensuring that marmalade-making continues, that tombolas are run, that bins are rinsed out and someone scrubs off the scummy bit round the rim of the bath. Someone has to do it. The world would spin off its axis and the species would die out if not.

Physically

Worst of all, you'll start to look like her. People tell you you're the spitting image of her. You too will get arsy with shop assistants and use words like 'inexcusable' and 'silly' and even 'common'. Yes, you will.

It's not just your body that is turning into *hers*. Your brain is

SIGNS YOU ARE TURNING INTO HER:

. . . .

You buy a tea towel from a National Trust shop with birds on.

You laugh and have a bit of an accident.

You like to get your pyjamas on before it is strictly necessary.

Sex is now on your to-do list – often in the carry-forward column.

A floral tablecloth gives you joy.

You remake beds because they don't come up to scratch.

Your mouth purses up with disapproval over something you would normally find trivial.

You're drawn to talcum powder.

You get fussy about your pillows, and feel the need to wash curtains, whereas before the thought would never have occurred to you.

You think about ringing the council.

You don't like driving at night.

Your pubes are thinning out.

You don't really understand James Bond films.

You've started buying *Good Housekeeping*.

You've got stubble everywhere.

You find yourself using the word 'cheerio'.

You like a hot-water bottle in the small of your back.

You buy some artificial flowers.

You spend a good five minutes searching for your keys in your bag every time you need them.

You think about food more than you think about sex. Sometimes you think about it when you're having sex.

You can't get drunk any more. Two glasses of wine and you've had it. If only they sold class-A drugs at Waitrose.

going all fuzzy around the edges too. People answer the phone and you forget who you've dialled. You have to write everything down, and then when you read it back you can't remember what it was you had to remember.

Matchmaker

Just like your own mother did, you become a matchmaker for your children, a Mrs Bennet, trying to marry her daughters off and get them settled, primarily so that you no longer have to worry about them so much. My daughters casually tell me about someone they've met at college or at work and my first question, if they sound successful and likeable, is: 'Are they married?' You see? It's happening to me too.

You can't fight this process, so you may as well make the most of it. Look on the bright side:

❀ You won't get so drunk you need to wee in the gutter.

❀ You won't feel the need to stick your bottom out of a stretch limo (actually, you never did) or be sick in the back of a taxi.

- You won't have to get chatted up by blokes who'll never ring you in the morning.

- You won't need to carry a condom.

- People may describe you as 'cantankerous' and 'feisty' (which is code for 'mean').

- You can get away with being really lazy. Tell everyone you can't get around like you used to, or you find the shops at Christmas are too much for you now, that way you can get other people to do it for you. Particularly if you have a daughter-in-law. Give out lists. Allocate tiresome jobs to her.

- You don't have to go camping ever again.

- You don't have to go to pop concerts …
  Or Alton Towers …
  Or skiing …
  Or hen nights …

- People might clap you when you tell them your age.

- You might even get a cat.

Eventually you will enter the next phase and turn into a proper old lady. You will no longer be old-young, more young-old. You'll have some toffees and a lot of tissues in your bag, you'll be saving string, and knitting really horrible jumpers. You won't miss being young. You have turned into your mother, but you don't care any more.

THINGS ARE WASTED ON THE YOUNG

1. Youth: You don't appreciate it when you're young. Once it's gone, you realise that when you thought you had big thighs, or you were worried about your visible panty line, or thought your nose was a bit of a honker … OMG this was as good as it ever was going to get and you didn't appreciate it!

2. Sex: Takes you ages to get the hang of it and then by the time you have the confidence to go up to a bloke and suggest some harmless rumpy-pumpy you've lost your figure or, worse, you've got pregnant, which means that from then on sex will only mean one thing: a displacement of more important sleep.

3. Sleep: Young people don't need sleep … as in they don't really do a fat lot to tire them out.

4. Education: All of a sudden I'm quite interested in Mary Queen of Scots and I'd like to win a trivia quiz, whereas when I was young I would just have thought that a bit sad.

5. Ginger nuts: Anyone under thirty-five should not be allowed them on the grounds that they will not be appreciated and will waste precious resources.

6. orphanages: Many of us in our fifties would now both qualify and benefit from a place in an orphanage. Think of the housing we'd free up, and we could have midnight feasts and dorm fun and outings and lollipops and games of musical statues … we'd sing hymns and have uplifting assemblies every morning. On second thoughts, maybe old people's homes are just orphanages for grown-ups.

LOOK ON THE BRIGHT SIDE

s you get older and turn into your mother, you will develop new tricks, new hobbies:

Rubbish in all its forms is the number one hobby or displacement activity for the over fifties. All that time you spent on heavy petting you now spend dividing household waste into specially labelled receptacles for newspapers, cardboard, recycling (cans), recycling (plastic), bottles (green), bottles (clear), and garden waste. Then you spend ages carting it all to the tip, putting wheelie bins at the end of the drive and then bringing them back again. You might even splash out on a wheelie camouflager in pebble or autumn leaf effect, or invest in a wheelie freshener.

Once you've rinsed it, sorted it, labelled it and loaded it into the car you can treat yourself to a trip to the tip. Trips to the local tip for the over forties are as good as sex. You load the car up with all the crap that has been cluttering up your spare room and your life, and come home feeling purged. It's like a really good shit.

Composting is the hobby you graduate to after ordinary recycling, since composting is recycling vegetables. To the uninitiated, composting means chucking leftover veg in a big plastic container outside the kitchen door. To the compost enthusiast, composting is a way of life; there are books on it, blogs on it, entire evening class courses on it, telling you exactly how to turn and aerate and mulch down your compost so that you can spread it on your borders or your allotment and feel really smug about it. I spent two years putting my vegetable peelings into my compost maker, sprinkling it each time with compost pellets that are supposed to hurry along the decomposition process, only to discover that when I came to shovel it out of its little drawer at the bottom for spreading I was basically just spreading the contents of my kitchen bin, with entire meals still visibly recognisable even after standing for two years. The smell nearly knocked me out.

Bonfires like composting, they get you outdoors, which for people who have turned into their own mothers is of vital importantance. There is nothing I like more than having a really good clear-out in the garden, and starting a bonfire. I love the smell, and I could watch the flames for hours. Sometimes, when no one is looking, I do. I pull up a horrible plastic chair, make myself a mug of tea, wrap up warm and just watch it. Euphoria would be a Twix at the same time. You see how easy to please women are when they have morphed into their mothers and given up the kicking and screaming in protest?

There are more wicked hobbies I've developed now. I like giving the eye to blokes in their seventies, really gnarled old boilers in anoraks with virtually no hair, who have been sent into town to do some errands with a silly shopping basket or a pull-along Scotch trolley. I like really giving them the come-on. Stare at them. Wink, if I have to. They'll do a double-take, look over their shoulder to check you mean them. They might blush, or they might give you a nice big smile or let you in at the car park queue. Be careful if they're driving or have a pacemaker – it could just be the last straw and might send them over the edge. On the other hand, fuck it: they'll die happy.

SOME TIPS FOR THE WOMAN WHO HAS TURNED INTO HER MOTHER

How to look ten years younger in a jiffy

❀ Go up a decade. The joy of this is that, not only will you look ten years younger, you'll feel ten years younger too. Spend as much time as possible with people who are at least a decade older than you, join the old biddies on the sit-down chairs by the till at M&S. They will be overjoyed at having someone young in their midst; they'll be delightful, listen to your every word, ask you where you got your outfit from. You might even be chatted up by some old boy with a pair of braces and a high-waisted pair of easy-care slacks. Who cares? You'll be chatted up. Enjoy it. Luxuriate in it.

❀ Coach trips or quilting groups could be a good idea for the same reason. It will be rejuvenating. You'll come home with a spring in your step, feeling younger, more alive. If you are forty, sneak into the over-fifties session in the pool. Watch how the women will look at you, wondering how your skin is so good and how you manage to fend off the cellulite; watch as men with hairy shoulders and knobbly knees eye you up and wistfully remember how much they enjoyed younger women.

❁ Dawdle. Hold younger people up – that hurts them more than anything.

❁ Pretend you can't find your change.

❁ Feign dementia. They will put you on buses and offer to carry your shopping.

❁ Pretend to be a frail, helpless old lady. Ask the local scout troop for help and get your house spring-cleaned from top to bottom. They will write off your mean donation as senile dementia.

❁ Join a flower-arranging class.

❁ Wear things that fit and are comfy.

❁ Let standards drop. Clean the house twice a year. Use the same pan twice in a row.

❁ Clean the kitchen floor only when it is a health hazard.

❁ Drink gin at lunchtime and fall asleep in front of *Cash in the Attic*. Everyone else does.

EMPTY NESTS

The apples have appeared on the trees, there's a chill in the air and the sun is starting to lose its heat. These portents spell one thing: time to go back to school. You run through a mental checklist: shoe fittings in John Lewis, gingham dresses ironed for the first few sunny weeks back before the winter uniform kicks in, name tags, syllabuses, reading books, times tables charts, parents nights … Except, one year it all stops. All of a sudden your life is no longer defined by the school year. The school years are over.

When I was a young mum very old ladies would come up to me and say, 'It goes in a flash, enjoy it while you can.' While I knew they were genuine, I didn't really get it and enjoyment wasn't really achievable on a day-to-day basis with two kids under five. But now my nest is empty, I am that old girl, and have found myself saying the very same thing to young mothers I meet on the Tube or in parks. I can't help it. I look enviously at their squidgy toddler with chubby little wrists and rosy cheeks – which was the phase I liked most: when they first giggle and smile at you and (here's the important bit) love YOU unconditionally. When they still like you, they still want to hold your hand in public and listen to what you have to say because they think you know stuff …

Well, when I say I look enviously at them, I mean it only

theoretically. The last thing I'd want now is a toddler to wear me out all day and displace all my new-found me-time. What I do think is, gosh, where did all that time go? Now my two are grown up, the nest is empty, and people half-heartedly ask me at the till, 'Are you collecting the school tokens?' As in, Well, I doubt it, but I have to ask.

You only really borrow your children, as the famous saying goes. And even though, when they were little, there'll have been times you'd have been delighted to hand them back, once they bog off to university you can't believe how much you miss them. Suddenly you've been dismissed without so much as a passing-out parade.

I suppose as mothers we have bits of preparation, little stages of practising letting go: they start nursery, their first day at big school, the first sleepover, the dreaded gap year (most mothers would cheerfully strangle whoever invented the gap experience), and then you pack them off to university, they buy their own flat, they get married, and for some poor mothers they move to the other side of the world. Thank goodness for Skype, and texting, and Internet cafés … But, let's face it, motherhood is something you need to enjoy every moment of while you have them on a daily basis.

Good luck with that, then …

The eldest one goes and it's devastating. For weeks afterwards you can't bring yourself to go into her room, or if you do you end up lolling about and moping on her bed, looking up at her posters and sniffing her dressing gown, or cuddling her soft toys. And if you're a total masochist you start to look at all the memorabilia you've been bunging in a drawer for the last eighteen years: mother's day cards, plaster-of-paris models, the postcard she sent you from her field trip to Devon in Year 4 (the one where you had to go and get her because she was so homesick). You count the days before you can go to visit her at university.

But little by little she takes with her more and more things from her room, until it's tidy. Now there are no cereal bowls under the bed or wet towels on the floor, but you'd give anything for it to be that way again. Even though it used to infuriate you. This is the spiteful bit about being a mother: it drives you mad at the time, but when it's gone you go into meltdown with the sheer loss of it. This seems very spiteful of God, especially given that most of us are battling the big M at the same time. Just as your hormones start going berserk, your role as a mother gets whipped from under your feet and you have to reassess the whole goddam thing.

Before you know it, the dynamics change to accommodate the emptiness. If you've got a younger sibling to cook some home-made soup for and sneak a kiss from once in a while, then you have to pull yourself together. For me, once it was just the three of us left in the house, there was something really quite snug about the arrangement. We missed the eldest Siena like hell, but there were fewer people to row about the TV remote, less pants to sort and more attention to go round. You adapt to having three table settings and you realise that you need to enjoy wholeheartedly the time the youngest is still at home because she too will soon be gone – so she gets away with comparative murder.

Then in a flash the second one's gone too, leaving you sick with worry and with no one to tuck up in bed or make a fuss of when they're ill. You're pleased for them, yes, but your own life needs major re-aligning to avoid insanity and the kind of moping and sulking that, as a mother, you used to warn against lest your face gets stuck like it. Alas, if you're sulking over an empty nest the chances are you're so old your face WILL get stuck like it. They say as you get older your face is a facemap of your life … Well, lady, you are going to have to pull yourself together and look on the bright side:

ADVANTAGES TO AN EMPTY NEST

✿ You will never have a cold bath again.

✿ Get real – looking after small kids was exhausting to the point of being life-shortening.

✿ You can let standards drop.

✿ You don't have to set an example at home – except when they come home mid-term.

✿ You can clean once a fortnight and no one will notice …
Actually, they never did notice.

✿ No one leaves the freezer door open.

✿ You can redecorate, knock down walls, clear out their rooms. (Moving on without a forwarding address might be taking this a step too far.)

✿ You can shag the old man during daylight hours and no one will know. OK, so this is very unlikely, but still – you could if you wanted to.

✿ You can holiday during the school term.

✿ Simple things will give you joy. Like being more in touch with the seasons.

✿ You'll have more time to make that patchwork quilt.

✿ Then again, dry white wine with a girlfriend might be more fun.

❀ Simple things will please you: you'll be drawn to travel kettles and housewifery and cake-related events of all kinds.

❀ You can run the village shop as a volunteer and shout at all the kids who come in after school to spend their pocket money on sweets.

❀ You can join jive classes and indulge in coffee mornings.

❀ You can go for an early morning swim.

❀ You no longer need to rush.

❀ You can make damson jam or chutney and put it into little jars with gingham covers on.

❀ You can let yourself go a bit and not worry about wearing things that are up to date. As if you haven't already been doing that for years.

LETTING GO/
SAYING GOODBYE

I vividly remember my mother being a sobbing mess the day I left for university with a car packed full of 10cc LPs and tins of Fray Bentos bake-in-the-tin pies. She was in a right old state for weeks leading up to it. I couldn't understand it at all. In fact, I remember thinking, What is it with HER? It's not like she's my boyfriend or anything. Now, of course, I so get it.

Saying goodbye to them as they head off into the big bad world is tough, really tough … and yet mothers have been doing this since time began. Imagine being a mother who had to say goodbye to a son for years on end when they went off to war, worrying whether they would come back alive. Fresher terms at university seem a doddle by comparison. Mind you, fresher weeks being what they are, it *is* a worry whether they will come back alive.

I think when the last one goes, mothers everywhere should be allowed to howl our heads off. In the first week of October, all empty-nest mothers should be encouraged to go and stand at the back door and just howl our heads off like dogs howling in the dead of night. We could do it collectively, or at four in the morning (most of us are awake anyway) when it really gets to us, and then we'd know that other people were feeling the same way and that we were not alone. That could be a way of legitimising the grief, making it OK to be really sad about your children leaving home instead of feeling such an idiot about it. Either that or all empty nesters should be given a month off – like maternity leave in reverse – to adjust, to spring-clean the house, to bog off to Spain with the old man and rediscover our sex lives, or take up stock-car racing (not sure which is more unlikely).

Only your fellow empty-nest mothers can really appreciate what you're going through, and your children are completely oblivious. For mothers, waving the children off as they leave home is so upsetting it is physically painful, but the children are oblivious to all that. Recently there's been a trend for parents to spend time with their children in fresher week at university to settle them in. Personally, I couldn't wait for my parents to get lost the moment I started unpacking my things for my new life at university. The longer they stayed, the more likely people were to realise what a shallow, uninteresting, ordinary person I really was – someone whose mother might have packed them a plastic mac or done them a packed lunch or sent them off into the world with a hot-water bottle encased in a knitted panda cover.

Mum Visits

My parents would always come and visit me at university and be early. Mum would say they'd be there at twelve and they'd roll up at eleven thirty. Half an hour – when you have to remove bottles, cigarettes, strange men from your room – is a long time. Her only saving grace was that, when she did visit, she'd bring her cleaning materials and a pinny.

There's nothing quite like your mother's level of cleanliness, particularly when you have left home and have your first baby. Suddenly the things she did that you detested when you were in your teens – like re-making your bed, putting your washing away and hoovering on a Sunday morning – are heaven indeed. Once you leave home, she can't stop herself. In she comes, looking round the room for dust, clutter and germs. She finds all three, even if you have spent the previous day cleaning your room or your flat from top to bottom. Her eyes will home in like a guided missile on any bits you've missed; mothers see skirting boards, the tops of pictures, behind and under furniture, and at the back of beds like no one else, without moving their heads or even their eyes. They know it, they sense it, they feel it in their bones. Once she is in cleaning mode, there is no stopping her. You turn your back for a minute to fetch her a mug of tea and she's started; she hasn't taken her coat off and already she's doing hospital corners. Out come the rubber gloves and cleaning fluid, and before you can stop her she has moved the bed out from the wall and – Wow! There are things down there that she wishes she hadn't seen.

Kitchens are the same. You might think you have spring-cleaned, but you haven't done *under* the washing-up bowl, and you haven't bleached (you don't even know about bleach). A brisk session of mum-cleaning and your swing bins are bleached and rinsed out, cupboards are wiped, and germs are annihilated. Your kitchen is mum clean. And you like it. Admit it: you like it.

Certainly standards drop at mission control when the nest empties. Now that there's just the two of us, we've been known to eat straight out of the saucepans, we can make a cabbage last a couple of days, eat cereals for supper and no one bats an eyelid. The other thing that happens is that couples tighten their belts; they realise all of a sudden that they are heading for retirement and as such need to keep a close eye on their spending. That, and they are now paying rent for two teenagers who have left home. Empty nesters collect coupons and actually redeem them at the till in the supermarket (parents with children at home would have zero chance of achieving this), which allows them to blow money on big things instead – they take Caribbean cruises in February and blow their savings on a kitchen that won't get ruined by children.

Bizarrely, just as my house is looking like a neat new pin and I have all the time in the world to straighten scatter cushions, I have developed an increasing indifference to it. I can only assume that my control issues over tidiness and everything having its place when the kids were at home were my way of persuading myself that I was doing a good job of motherhood.

The fact that you've decided to move on and get your own life doesn't mean that your children will be prepared for the consequences. They think they are, but all of us can remember calling our mothers after we left home with an emergency – such as needing them to post us our Ugg boots, or tell us what to do when a cake has sunk in the middle and they don't answer. And then they don't reply to your text – for goodness' sake, normally they reply to your texts with tragic punctuality. For God's sake, where is she, just when you need her? Mothers are not ALLOWED to be off duty, Not even when they are over seventy.

You might know that, mothers being mothers, even when the nest has emptied they don't stop kicking themselves for not being perfect mothers. They mither about what they did wrong. Once the hurly-burly of day-to-day mothering has come to an end, they realise how they could have done it better, and how much more they should have enjoyed it. This is all very well, but remember: at the time you were too busy putting up packed lunches or buying head-lice shampoo to enjoy it.

All those years when you lamented being so utterly exhausted you could barely climb the stairs at night, and now it's done. All tidied up and finished and you don't know what to do with yourself. If, like me, you have been a working mother, you start to wish you hadn't spent so much time away from them when they were still in (your) captivity. What were you doing, wasting precious mummy time being busy with spreadsheets and meetings and deadlines and trying to do everything at once? What were you thinking of? In my case, I can't even say to myself that I was doing something really important, since my day job has always been working in TV, which isn't really a proper job at all. That's one way of looking at it; the other way is to remember that as a working mother you at least have a job to fall back on when the kids move on. This can be seriously life- and sanity-saving, since you could otherwise find yourself sucked into doing the flowers for church or running the nearly new stand at the Easter Fayre, not to mention clogging your brain up with gardening clubs and joining the Women's Royal Voluntary Service, which surely is for trainee old ladies. But wait ... you are a trainee old lady.

Turning into your father

Once the kids have left and you have turned into your mother, phase two will be on its way. Namely turning into your father. I've started to get a little bit fussy about the state of my car, I'm drawn to a shammy leather, I listen to Elaine Paige and Neil Sedaka, I complain that people are standing in my light when I'm up a ladder, I huff and puff, I spend a bit of time choosing the right car parking space at Tesco's, I like a real hankie. I draw the line at military history books, but eventually I shall get a shed. I'm only sorry that I didn't hang on to his Gillette.

THE CONTENTS OF A MUM'S HANDBAG

(which has hundreds of compartments and zip-up sections, none of which are used – or if they are, there is no system)

Six used tissues

Used lumps of chewing gum in tissue, one of which has got stuck to the lining

Two Lipsyls, one with the top off

Baby wipes

An apple to tide her or someone else over

Extra-strong mints

Hand sanitiser

An iPod that hasn't been switched off properly and is flat

Sugar-free Polos

Nit comb

Keys – work keys, house keys, car keys – all sloshing around, always right at the bottom, and never put back in the same place

Phone – always right at the bottom, or in a compartment where she can't get to it fast enough when it rings

Purse bursting at the seams with receipts and money-off coupons now out of date

Reading specs tangled up in a scarf

A photo of her children ten years out of date

Her favourite lipstick in a zippy-up compartment

Her mother's disabled badge, which she uses occasionally (being careful to put a limp on)

Her make-up bag, which weighs a ton, even though she only uses one eyeliner, mascara and one lipstick

Calorie counter

A to-do list

A shopping list

A 'remember things' list

A diary

A Key Stage 3 Maths book (both children are KS2)

Calpol in a plastic bag so that if it leaks like it did last time it won't go everywhere

A biro that has run out of ink

An Interflora card from her husband which was sent five years ago

A place setting from a wedding

Earplugs

Nurofen

A tampon that has come undone. It's been that long.

AFTERWORD

I've written a book about motherhood – as it happens, just as my own kids were leaving the nest, and my own mother suddenly passed away. The process has underlined how precious mothering is. Now that my own full-time mothering is coming to an end, and my own mother has gone, I worry that I didn't slavishly praise my own mother every single day I had her. I thought she was as indestructible as her terrible rock-hard pastry, but she's gone, along with her limitless interest in everything I do. And life will never be the same again.

But we all know it's complicated. Mothers are utterly, irreplaceably vital to us, but it's probably just as well that mothers aren't perfect. They're bossy, controlling, annoying, all-seeing … and usually proved right. If they were perfect, they'd be unbearable.

My own mum taught me everything I know. Not mental arithmetic, or how to do isometric tests. Much more important things. She taught me how to tuck someone in on the sofa when they feel poorly, or take them up a bowl of home-made soup with a little eggcup and a flower in. She taught me how to love someone right down to the bottom of my toes. So let's hear it for motherhood; after all it literally makes the world go round.

Why mum is a mum in a million